A Restricted View
From Under The Hedge

(In The Springtime)

Published in the UK by
The Hedgehog Poetry Press
Coppack House, 5
Churchill Avenue
Clevedon
BS21 6QW

www.hedgehogpress.co.uk

Copyright © M Davidson 2018

The right of M Davidson to be identified as the editor of this work has been asserted by him in accordance with the Copyright, Designs and Patents Act 1988. All rights to the poetry within are retained by the individual authors.

Cover Image © Kanoe West

All rights reserved. No part of this publication may be reproduced, stored in or introduced into a retrieval system, or transmitted in any form, or by any means (electronic, mechanical, photocopying, recording or otherwise) without prior written permissions of the publisher. Any person who does any unauthorised act in relation to this publication may be liable for criminal prosecution and civil claims for damages,

A CIP Catalogue record for this book is available from the British Library.

ISSN: 2515-9313 (Magazine)
ISBN: 978-1-9996402-1-7 (Book Edition)

WAVING

From Under The Hedge

I have to say that I am slightly relieved to get the first issue of *A Restricted View From Under The Hedge* finished and into your hands, as it feels like it has taken far too long and to be totally honest I bore easily.

However, looking at the contents list I'm pleased that I didn't chase squirrels instead as I wouldn't be able to see so many fine poets, both in the poetry section and then in the articles and interviews too.

I won't embarrass myself by listing them, however much I want to, but if you have been following the web site and wondering why I keep using the word 'eclectic', I would imagine all is now clear, or soon will be when you get past this drivel and read the important part.

But, I'm the least interesting person at this party, so I'll leave you in peace and hopefully see you next time.

MD
February 2018

Poetry,

Chen Chen 9
M. Stone 10
D. M. Thomas 12
Peter J. King 14
Phil Hawtin 19
Robert Sheppard 20
Charlotte Begg 25
Zoe Mitchell 26
Sophie Hannah 28
Eileen Myles 30
Sarah Bigham 31
Tawnya Renelle 32
S.A. Leavesley 34
Bill Herbert 35
Jane Burn 36
Nick Toczek 38
Eileen Carney Hulme 39
Johanna Boal 40

Kristin Garth 41
Rachel Burns 42
Georgina Titmus 45
Diana Devlin 46
Brian Docherty 47
Megan Falley 48
Moniza Alvi 49
Joe Williams 50
Jonathan Jones 52
Beth McDonough 53
Nigel Kent 54
Sonia Davies 56
Melissa Fu 60
Sanjeev Sethi 62
Martin Malone 64
Mimi Khalvati 66
Chen Chen 67

Articles,

Brian Patten *Talks With Eileen Carney Hulme* 69
Alison Lock *Revealing The Odour of the Earth* 74
Penny Rimbaud *What Passing Bells* 78
Paul Moss *Poem I Wish I'd Written* 87
Matt Duggan *One Million Tiny Cuts* 88
Patricia Oxley *Talks Acumen* 92
Charlotte Begg *Talks Eye Flash Poetry* 102
Penny Rimbaud *America and How!* 106
Sandra Beasley *Count The Waves* 109
S.A. Leavesley *How To Grow Matches* 111
Isabelle Kenyon *This Is Not A Spectacle* 117
Isabelle Kenyon *Please Hear What I'm Not Saying* 120
Sandra Beasley *The Building of a Collection* 123
The Road To Clevedon Pier 126
    Winner -   *Victoria Richards* 127
    Runners-up - *Sarah Thomson* 130
        & *Matt Duggan* 133
A.P. Middleton *Deus Ex Machina* 135
Moose *Postcards From The Hedge* 138

CHEN CHEN

Les Cloches de Genève

after Franz Liszt

dear friend   in the cursive wind
      dear face   italicized
   by snow   your bright   punctuation
       of me   at 2
3 a.m.   dear
   echo   bell-filled
footnote   your best
            & worst
         piano lessons
                holding hands
    friend
  I do not know
          how to miss you
   but I do

M. STONE

Who Could Bear That Burden?

The old dog paces, aimless,
forgetting where she is, forgetting
herself and us, but she keeps eating
and drinking, drifting into fitful sleep
until the day she doesn't.
Then we know it's time.

On that day, we think of our own deaths,
the shadow forever edging our vision,
the mute companion present at the table.

We know our bodies, dependable
bags we cart around, will betray us,
seams weakening before the bottom

drops out altogether, spilling what's left
into a useless pile for loved ones to tidy up
and then tuck out of sight.

I weep as you cradle the dog. She is wrapped
in her favorite blanket, the cheery yellow one
with various Beatrix Potter characters.
The vet administers the needle, delivering
a peaceful death.

On the way home, you are rigid
and wide-eyed in the driver's seat.
"I'm terrified," you say, "I'll end up
in that state with no one to help me."

I nod, empty of comforting platitudes.
My reply, mouthed behind closed lips,
is bell-clear in my head, so loud
I wonder if you can hear:

*Do you see why I wouldn't wish
existence on anyone? Do you now understand
those days when I'd give back my own
if I could?*

D. M. THOMAS

From Shadow Sonnets, *a sequence*

A hundred violent quarrels

A hundred violent quarrels there distilled,
My kitchen table emulates my heart;
Staring at me over your Scotch, you held
Interrogations, your consummate art.

I'd joke that you had a Gauleiter's skill,
Finding my weak points, exposing all my lies;
At 5 a.m. we could be at it still,
Narrowed with rage, your lovely grey-green eyes.

I'd stand to go to bed. 'I haven't done!'
I'd sit again. My sister wanted me
To dump what had such cigarette burns on.
A new one? Never! This was our history,

Our battlefield; we couldn't tear apart;
She might as well have said, Transplant your heart.

Grief overwhelming

Grief overwhelming: will it never be done?
I sobbing, stumbling, through the creekside mud
And pools from April's rain, under weak sun,
A wash of blue sky; the Moresk trees in bud

But all I see is you – transformed to this,
A load with which none other can compare,
But further weighed by all I did amiss.
How unbearably plentiful our ashes are.

I pour out you, my love. It makes no sense.
My dear accuser, my fierce advocate
When others dared attack me. We were immense
Together, passionate in our love and hate.

   The urn, at last, is emptied. So it must be.
   My sobs won't stop. That heron echoes me.

After Shakespeare's sonnets 24, 35.

PETER J. KING

Larkin from the Festival Platforms

Miles
    balance dispelled
        rebarbative applause
            hard and energetic

Monk
    screwball significance
        scored for swings
            hollowly fruity

Miles and Monk
    manoeuvring an ear
        strong and bothered
            wavering, hard ragbag

Carrion Comfort

1
wrenching from the middle, going outward,
tearing from the centre, not expanding,
but leaving the centre empty, just leaving it
empty, just leaving it, leaving him, leaving
it empty
      and there's such a thin skin left
around now, such a molecule of thickness slick
around the nothing nature can't do anything
about because it's not there, because there
isn't a middle, because just not there and you
can't take a hole away, you can't take it
                                  not
ending it. anyway, there's a bit somewhere on
the surface (it's all, of course, surface) that
firmly believes, he firmly believes that it
may get better, he firmly denies that it will
get better, it can't keep from bursting, it
keeps from bursting, it doesn't burst, he
                                he
darks; he finds darkness inside, and even that's
translation, even just such a fine void.
anyway, too late

2
there was a quickening elevation, one bell, then
three, kneeling, empty, but he firmly believes
                              trans-
itions from this journey to a longer or damper
changing, and the inside shows through his eyes;
his mouth he keeps shut, but the eyes aren't
deep, but not even depth applies, only the rims
and then
            she crosses to the window, and in between
the double panes of glass a fluid drives up and
down, the view seen now through clear glass, now
through a(n almost membranous) red liquid that
shifts with thermal-chivvied shapes and bubbles,
now not seen at all because she's closed his eyes;
it's a hinged pain he holds now, just fluttering,
opening
            flies, and falls, and tried to flutter
weakly up again
                  teeth clamped

3
it's a scent, now; learning about numbers and
time, learning about the nighttime, and how he
travels then, because you don't have to keep
his mouth clamped tight to shield her, what she
left or made or
                    sometimes on his knees, sometimes
he kneels and slows down a bit, and just a hint
of winter feels his limbs; his outside never
wrinkles, pressing outward from the centre they
left or made or
                    young masks in a small night-
storm ("you trying to say something?") but
quickening his dark guts, his black guts, his
nothing inside, he's nothing inside, just watch
the skin billow, just watch the two tears form,
dribbling down from cornea to heel on the inside,
trickling down, freezing
                          leaving it empty, just
leaving it, the centre, just going out, wrenching
from the middle

Rictus

        mirror
        in the bathroom
        steamed up and reflecting
        little clearly — just the bright red
    of fresh blood, the mirror's surface splattered
with the first spray as the razor
    sliced at skin beneath the
        pale face in the
            mirror

PHIL HAWTIN

Standing Out In The Crowd

There's more to rooks than unrelenting 'kaah'.

There's the ancestral home. No bland
Easter Island heads on the edge
of oblivion or deserted stone chambers,
but nests rebuilt each year with twigs reused,
fresh, or stolen – the game flock species play.

By not only plumage or 'call' do you 'fly' tall.

From on high, they look down at the water-filled
drainage ditch, haunt of heron, and the River Nar,
it's banks sloping down from the dog-walker bald path
to this chaos, this jumbled andiron of land
between the road, trees and bushes,
and houses on the low ridge.

Land too wet for telegraph poles to stay upright,
too misshapen to be much use to man, but grass
enough to conceal mice and voles from owls, almost.

There's more to rooks than eyeing the sky
at the passing retreat of swift and swallow,
before autumn winds sweep nests away.

More than a mass Hitchcock fantasy,
a billowing cloak of darkness grasping
the wind in quivering feather-tips,
to descend onto the household waste site,
neighbouring fields' harvest detritus,
among unconcerned horses, or to perch on pigs.

Pigs understand there's more to each rook.

ROBERT SHEPPARD

Breakout

didn't think

it would be like this green murk
slanted light catches the national fish basking
just below the surface black lengths wait
sluggish broody & autistic stirring things up

for a jape the men see where
to cast their bait vote British now
it's an antonym to paki spat in
the street but the fish rest unmoved

as a terror truck ploughs into a
celebrant crowd its national day 100s of
miles away the continent we no longer
belong to our sympathy tempered by autonomy –

they've got our country back for us
and now they want it for themselves

twitter diplomatics

break shaft noises back and forth hold
hands up winking tank lit black forces
exchanging fire to drop over mid-rank chains
whose masterminded orders for those vasty super strollers

newswires unconfirm huge whichway swerving in the
headlights and clubs' high pillared floodlit facetime
in streets just glimmers on peppered iphones
chiefs on lower downs from downy drips

they are moving complete glued radio blackouts
Attaturk tanks on streets promise soldiers waving
in slanted darkness talk of confused blondes
licking microphone ice creams in slapping shame

for healing gunfire on the helicopter parliament
a secular bloodshot crowd flips every gunshot

chaos limbed

tinged by heavenly vision tingled darts folded
from ambrosia into utopian innards of gospel
bring back regrexit deserts hanging conspiracy fire
against steady English rain watch infective eye
that cannot be lidded free of cleft
bobbing head reciting poems about nothing flickable
deceit at quotidian world puzzles turned cockpits
to sticky pools of pleasure herbicidal bitterness
re-absorbed into body ink dried into pattern
a loud table of word-folds a
'French' *entrée* wilful as a *New European*
headline carnival passing girls in feathers twirling
atremble to the beat while the heat
lifts its alien rhythm to polonium cocktails

fuck the

pigmeat resting against the untended blade blandishments
of the apparatchik! speak post-truth unto powerlessness
wormholing exits within Brexit for the tweets
of the hopeful minutes and matters arriving

I've forcefed my kidnapped evil poets watercress
scrumpy and their own bad verses until
they relinquish their copyrights and I release
them tonguetied back into the wordless wild!

failure buried in a national moment infectious
as aspiration in palpable echoes of following
his workplace soviet outvotes my replete un-employability

the post-factual world lies at my feet
but I am wearing somebody else's boots
and my toes are twitching to kick!

breaking point

pointed out they all broke out of
wisdom into classic eurocratic distrexit data and
cobweb dusters thick with Londonism sneeze the
Briggering actioned by our slippy doggy do-dos

microdrone and sphericam catch the pinched elegance
cranes swing over procurement and Calais searchlights
polyglot polymaths tax a multilingual driver uncertainty
outweighs expertise they happy-houred to him

wriggling out of clown suits while offsite
unicorns gallop offshore patriots pencil conspiracy in
booths or coin puritan Corbynista temperance tempers
bumpily depicting rammed roundabouts with no exits

lorries at the border queue for inspection
(my passport to Ealing has been rescinded)

CHARLOTTE BEGG

Stamp

Slick eyes resting for kicks on sand dunes
that are not entirely sand whatever sand attempts to be-

(a make shift cell? A barricade of fractured bones?)
I cannot tell you how it comes to be

but the eyes do
they do an injustice to you and

Other amateur makers shifting
trying to climb

salt dusted bones bleached
from gamma rays in the pursuit of whelved stars

that are not entirely stars whatever stars attempt to be-
(mimicking swifts? A thrush's dipped beak?)

I'll hold on to that cheek on cheek
never letting slip the inked-out punches kissed.

ZOE MITCHELL

Camhanaich

camhanaich (n) [pronounced kav'-an-ach.]
A Scots-Gaelic word meaning the half-light of dawn or dusk.

At first light,
before the day can begin
its busy work of particulars,
a golden gesture greets
those who meet the possibility of morning.
The sun will warm the journey
to the place you must be.
Tread with care through the dissipating haze.

At last light,
after the day has called time
on its own relentless march,
a silver salute hails
those not yet at rest on the quiet, tired earth.
The moon will light you to a place
where you can sleep.
Lie back now and watch the blintering stars.

The Augur in Autumn

He wants to learn what the birds might teach him.
The hum that vibrates in a vacated skyline
speaks of the season. Glossy backs turn from cold
as the long tail of a taken path streams

across the sky. He looks for the not-yet
departed, hears the sooty-feathered scream
caught in roosted arches and vaulted rooftops
and tastes aerial plankton and raindrops.

He soars at dusk, sees through peeping new eyes
to chart the years ahead – above the clouds,
across an ocean – feels himself sling-shot
into the wind in search of better weather.

A pierced call – leave one home for another.
Eat. Mate. Sleep. Remain in continuous flight.

SOPHIE HANNAH

The Means

Lie down. Do not be counted.
Relax. You still exist.
When the attack is mounted,
you won't be on the list.

They'll look, but they won't find you
near where they won't find me.
I will be right behind you,
knowing where not to be:

where ends are falsely padded,
where friends turn into means.
Don't let yourself be added
to the great hill of beans.

I wasn't four or forty;
I won't be forty-nine.
I don't care who's been naughty
or who has crossed a line -

how could I, when I fidget
and laugh hysterically?
My name is not a digit.
You cannot count on me.

After Edna St Vincent Millay

My candle burns at both ends.
I cannot put it down.
I'm asking for my money back
next time I go to town.

EILEEN MYLES

Kitchen/Holidays

The kettle
whistling

& I'm peeling
an orange I'm going
to finish
in the
air
of this
wild horn

and I splash
the boiling
water into
the French
press

splattering
water
splashing
grains

I'm such
an oaf

I wanted
to be
here
with you.

SARAH BIGHAM

Oscillating independence without a trial

For she is but the trustee of the morning,
prowling through velvet-laden air
while you turn and snore and
drool and choke, your heart beating
steadily or stopping in place.
She roams the night,
the wee early hours
when dreams and hopes
meet, possibilities aplenty.
Do not succumb to the draw of
slumber, for then the magic
ends. And ends. And ends
again.

TAWNYA RENELLE

Alive

Conception

Nobody wants to think about their parents having sex

but I think about mine
because I wonder how my mom slept with a man who hit her.

Pregnancy

I asked my mom
       if she thought about aborting me.

an unplanned bastard

       What is the female word for Bastard?

illegitimate

She told me it was never an option.

I think she might have lied, worried about hurting my feelings.

I would be proud to have been almost aborted,

that my mom had a choice.

Maybe it wasn't an option because I was hope.

A baby that might end violence.

Birth

but I didn't.

I wonder about how much of a disappointment it was to her.

S.A. Leavesley

Zen and the Art of Cycle Maintenance *

Firstly, beware of others' forecasts –
shower or shine. Never let them
lend you their cloud, or silver linings.

Check for yourself daily. Pay attention
to the small parts, avoid over-oiling;
you've more than one chain to maintain.

When you pedal against your shadows'
competition, remember bike, body and brain
are thin frames blustered by strong winds.

Potholes will hold puddles, even on dry days;
tyre tracks gutter long roads. Each breath
you take is thickened by particles of loss.

The weather that freights this air to you
is heavy with the world's shed atoms.
Inhaled, ions of everything float

inside you: dust-like, star-like,
ready primed with light and dark,
as you push faster and harder

trying to grasp life's brief sparkle...
Remember now to never-never
believe your own forecasts.

* 'The real cycle you're working on is a cycle called yourself.'
Robert M. Pirsig, Zen and the Art of Motorcycle Maintenance

BILL HERBERT

Portokalia

The stickiness of juice is everywhere like light
on the oranges' attendants: olivewood board
and knife, blue plastic cup with its pointed dome
of radial serrations that requires a name
more exact than 'press'. There are other shapes
we live with as wordless as how many
of these hills' hundred variations on χόρτα?

Amid which the picking: stalked pairs that won't
be separated; the cutting into and the interiors:
pipless, twin elder suns that hiss their essence,
zest from the ζέστη. You press with increasing force,
one palm, two - even both topped with your chin -
then the whole gentle weight of the upper body,
as the lover presses upon the breastbone.

Sound of the gushets releasing settles the un-
guessable yield, meagre or an excess of giving;
spent halves piling in a sort of soft ossuary,
all skull-tops and no jaws. Fill and clink
small glasses that deserve a small silver tray
to set them down on; four lips touching glass,
reluctant at this sharpness before such sweetness -

as hot, almost, as raw garlic. Then, thirst as eagerness,
the animal finally given permission to drink.

Portokalia (πορτοκάλια)—orange; χόρτα—wild greens; ζέστη—heat; gushet-segment (Scots).

JANE BURN

Angels, Space Stations, Cows

The flowers that closed through the passing
of another night break their deep-slept buds,
open to dew, to the lace of tracked snails.

A fat sun crowns the hill, a baby's head
rising to the sky's milk – it climbs the scribble
of waking trees, matches the moon's

still-chalked circle. *I am day*, she tells
the woken Earth, her voice a pleasure of rays
sung to rooftops. The Sunday bell cries

its iron tears, clapper like a lobbed tongue,
heart of sound called from under its dome.
Birds make calligraphy, brush-tipped wings

pushing them further away from ground.
The mourn of crows, the happy *chit*
of sparrows – their gram-weight hearts

and tiny bladders of lung swelled with song,
strawy bones filled with nothing. Their flight given
to air, clouds shaking free of dawn grey – above

them, angels and space stations, dust and
asteroid lumps. A sticky ring of human prayer,
lodged in troposphere. A distant farm, breaking

its gum of land is edged in poached mud
as pied cows tread the periphery, brew
lakes of pasty skim, bob their dehorned heads.

Roadkill

Oh, my broken heart! My broken thing! I kneel –
do not feel the stones marking their rhombus shape
to my pressed flesh, look about for help. Oh, my baby,
oh, the mess of my poor, poor love! I have never seen
this creature up so close – have not, till now been blessed

with this honour. I am stunned by its magic, even as
I see its hurt. Among the lobbed plastic, crushed cans,
one filthy cork-heeled summer shoe lies a myth,
on its side, panting. What should I do? Leave it?
You must walk away from wild lives, let Nature take

the souls she will – yet forgive me for reaching out.
My thought was to scoop you up – tend to you. How?
Do I have a towel? Who could mend this tangled scrap?
I reach out a hand – it does not flinch, just turns
a rosin eye to mine, spot of pupil massive with fight

or flight. I want to make it okay. My fingers reach
its body – it will either run or stay. I never felt anything
so soft, as if it doesn't exist, as if it's made of fables.
As if I went to touch it and missed. I just want to get it
off the road – the next car along will burst it like a bleb.

It sits up, tries to flex a pair of ruined legs. Then seems
to mend, slowly tilts its way into a nearby field,
turns back toward me, wilts to the plough. I return later
to check, to follow from where it bled. I see that it
managed to get a little further out. The hare is dead.

NICK TOCZEK

Scars

These are the regions of hatred and pain
Pieces of days that we cannot contain
This is the burning returning again
Wounds which have healed yet their shadows remain

After the cleansing there'll still be a stain
Sins are forgiven but grudges ingrain
Tattooed forever deep inside your brain
Faraway songs with a snagging refrain

Atmospheres lingering long after rain
Items of evidence buried in vain
Surfacing shrapnel our bodies retain
Devils deputed to drive us from sane.

EILEEN CARNEY HULME

Self-discovery and Cappuccino

At the next table they are discussing angels, nothing
unusual about that, here outside the Phoenix café in
Findhorn. Conversation moves on to the loan of *Dali's
Christ of St John of the Cross* from Scotland to London.
I have stood beneath that painting many times, I have
stood there with you, I have stepped back, moved to the left
to the right. Flew with you to Florence to pursue a love
of Renaissance, cried at the prospect of *Primavera*.
I go back to flicking through a book on Chakras, first
purchase on the road to finding me, consider the cleansing
and balancing of mine. I close my eyes as if to meditate
visualising the colours, should I start at my crown or my root.
I haven't got that far in the book. A northern sun settles
on my eyelids, pretending yellow, my search for inner-peace
punctuated by thoughts of last night's film *Eat Pray Love*
Julia Roberts eating spaghetti, Javier Bardem as my *tour guide*.

JOHANNA BOAL

What Else Can I Say

It's such an affair watching,
but I'm never too sure
what to look at first,
facing physical attractiveness
golden cleavage of Whitesands Beach.
But then my back is in contrast
ruffled, green collar, unbuttoned at the neck
makes the squiggly, diamond of a cove
the Pembrokeshire coasts.

KRISTIN GARTH

Flutter

Estate enchantment on a lake, a lass
extends a finger, her mistake, to moths.
A moonlit flutter does disguise their mass,
a swarm, not butterflies, as maidens caught.

Surprise that lands with chestnut wings on hands
it covers, mottled message sings. Its tale
of death, disease and woe. Its dark demands,
details she should not know become her veil.

Surrounded, followed fearsome flaps, human
contact reduced to shrieks and gasps. The beasts
she wears are tragedy. Their flitter fans
all misery — from dark wings, no release.

A solitude of secrets insects utter
since she first saw death in darkness flutter.

RACHEL BURNS

Chainsaws

(after Les Murray)

We watch The Texas Chainsaw Massacre
at a friend's house on Betamax, her parents are out
it is the bloodiest film I ever saw
severed limbs and screaming girls
the sound of the blade ripping through
the girl's dress.

Coming ready or not!

We scream, hiding behind cushions on the couch
screaming at the girl - *run - run - run- hide.*
Here comes Leatherface!
Our screams drown out her screams,
the sound of the rip roaring chainsaw
makes our toes curl, our flesh crawl.

Teenage Pregnancy

I went into labour
and had to go to the payphone
and phone for the ambulance
the ambulance men were jokey
and said did I want to stop
off at Morrisons and do my shopping
I laughed but didn't find it funny
cos I had no money and hadn't
eaten in like a week.

At the hospital the midwife
made it clear that she thought
having a baby at eighteen meant
I was a bad person and she wasn't
about to waste her valuable time
when there were other mothers
more deserving.

She left me in a room for twelve hours
came back and said the baby's
in distress- we have to get it out now.
They pinned me to the bed
and put an intravenous drip in my arm
and hooked me up with drugs
and I got scared and screamed the place down.

The midwife complained
about having to deliver babies
to silly teenage girls who didn't go to
anti- natal classes and didn't do
what they were told.

They took my baby into another room
and I thought it was dead. They were gone
for a while but came back and swaddled
him and put him in a Perspex box
at the other side of the room.
I was too scared to look at him.

GEORGINA TITMUS

The Hadal Zone

Unfathomably alien, darkly
devoid; bioluminescences
bloom.

Maritime miasma, spawning
desolation; abyssal gametes
fuse.

Primordial nomads, enraptured by
depth; freakshow exquisite
in gloom.

                     Blind mouths feed.

DIANA DEVLIN

Barefoot love

Our love sizzles like a skyful of summer.
It tingles on the tongue,
as shocking as a bee sting
on the lips, cries *See me!*

Our love demands to be worn,
like a tiara in greedy gleamfulness,
precious and weighty, its load
pain perfect.

Our love is a magnificent mare
that refuses to be shod,
that gallops through horizons, like
a devil playing God.

Our love walks barefoot.
Beware.

BRIAN DOCHERTY

Hotel Delirium, Buenos Aires

I wanted a quiet vacation, what I got
was thunderstorms, invites to a Polo Club

and a winning Loto ticket bookmarking
Revelation 1:3 in the bedside Gideons Bible.

After that, my credit was good all over town,
I was offered a diamond-encrusted iPhone

by the night porter, the keys to a Bugatti
from the concierge, a case of Quilmes bock,

a micro pig & a bucket of live crabs for a beach
bbq the staff would organise in my honour.

Then I was told I had to be resident or citizen
to claim; local bank, no cash, no transfer

to a UK bank, but for *un honorario, señor* . . .
my Spanglish gave out at that point.

Later I found the teddy bear, a vintage Steiff
with his own silk pyjamas & name tag.

His owner turned up next morning;
she didn't care about the Lottery ticket.

I offered her a deal - marry me, then claim
the prize; joint account, you get Ruben back.

Now, Ruben & I sit in a cafe opposite the bank.
If I get my travel expenses, we both go home

MEGAN FALLEY

Said The Gun To The Woman On Her Way To Planned Parenthood

What pisses me off is that you are the one
they call murderer. Treat me like a thing
to protect, and you get to be the monster.
Like it was not me who shot
up the club and gave new meaning
to a last dance. Not me who sat back
in my hotel room and turned a music festival
into one long scream. Not me who entered
a classroom of children learning ABC's
and punctuation and taught them
how I. End. A sentence. They say you think
you can play God, but in this country, I am God.
So they'll argue that I'm innocent,
closets of suits pledging allegiance, writing clean,
crisp, amendments. While you do nothing
but choose to save your life and you get riots
outside the clinic, a bomb in the belly
of a dumpster? Tell me, what have you been
aiming for? Joy? Freedom? A body
that is yours? Let's be clear.
I'm the only one of us
who is not pro-life
here.

MONIZA ALVI

No Comfort

'I' said the dove
'I mourn my love'.
  Who killed Cock Robin?

The dove pines
in her cramped corner.
Chief comforter,

I offer her some seed-cake.
Caraway seeds, Persian cumin –
she pecks them all out.

They're small and ribbed
and warmly aromatic
but they don't help.

We gathered around him,
before and after –
though none of us,

not even the fly
saw him die.

JOE WILLIAMS

Fake News

It was an incredible night,
completely unexpected.
It started as a normal Friday
down at the pub.
But Kate Winslet was there,
leaning on the bar
drinking bright blue cocktails through a straw.
She smiled at my witty remark.
We got chatting.

Then who should show up but Brian Cox -
the professor,
not the actor -
who turns out to be a friend of Kate's,
and a very interesting bloke
when he's not blabbing on about string theory.

And I didn't even realise it was
two months and seventeen days
since you said you didn't love me.

They were going to a party
and invited me along.
One of those fancy showbiz dos
at a posh hotel, with free champagne
and David Guetta DJing.
Madonna was there,
and Alan Bennett.
You wouldn't have thought it would be his sort of thing
but he was loving it.

And not for one second did I think about you,
or wish you could be there too.
I was having far too much fun
with the Latvian ambassador
and the blonde one out of the Saturdays.

In the morning, when I got back home,
I heard the news
and laughed,
because I knew it couldn't possibly
be true.

JONATHAN JONES

The B movie Marriage of Figaro

Mozart laughs
manic as an axe murderer
in his poverty

a higher intelligence -
There!

eight tentacles beneath
his shabby wig.

The pink ooze slithers
and gains pace
as the crowd goes crazy.

The urge to escape

that was not born of fear,
but more the expectancy -
of happiness like Figaro

singing to his marriage bed,

not a sense of entitlement
as much as

the
wheel
of a horse
drawn cart

behind a screen of loud applause.

BETH MCDONOUGH

Cutting rhubarb

Cutting rhubarb slant through stems; the knife rasps sharp obsesses.
Stems overcome threats
of a cropped Scots stewing – bens
contour on scales, heap careless into bowls.

Snow sugar this over its own weight
then tart with a ginger-heavy hand.
Let that soak into the night
under wraps. Fast boil

for a quick-set jam, fill
sufficient hot jars. Who'll
spread all this? Who gives a damn?
Untended, rhubarb just shoots off.

NIGEL KENT

Empty Nest

I found it under
the cherry tree:
a starling's nest,
abandoned by its
rowdy residents
who took their leave
two weeks before,
writing farewell
in cursive script
across the pale,
vellum sky.

In cradled fingers
I take it to the house,
and lay it by
her pile of post:
something to show
and tell when she
returns at end of
term...

...which seems so
long to wait
and feelings that
I'd cased
and stored
with carrier bags
of cuddly toys
and old school books
strain the
catches.

I see her, still,
standing on
the hostel steps,
half-turned,
hand raised,
and her last
whispered bye
evaporating
from the clouded
glass
and remember how
returning home
I lost my
way.

SONIA DAVIES

The Last Bus to Trimsaran.

They are having fun by the bucketful;
 those hordes having heaps of jolly japes,
joining in the songs, the wrong words are
streaming out from those red-glossed lips,
shaking those black velvet hips, sipping cheap wine,
their minds befuddled by Black Russians, Bulmers and Baileys.
Billy Bunter bosses, belching out boozy breath like jovial
        Welsh dragons,
exuding happy hospitality; benevolence personified.
The Christmas Night Out at the gastro pub .
Yee hah!

Inhibitions are left at the door, the paper hats worn with
carefree abandon, they all reckon it is so bloody funny!
Hysterically humorous, in fact.
Managers mingle lasciviously with teenage temps
who are totally exempt
from paying their way tonight. But they know the score.
Keep smiling and giggling at the fat old bore and he will cough
        up more and more
and buy them drinks galore.....
A Cosmopolitan?
A glamorous cocktail for the gorgeous girls.
Fabuloso!

The cold rain outside makes no impression on the seasonal cheer,
whisky-filled eyes, shop-bought mince pies and Blackberry lies
of the office staff.
Unaware of the housewife waiting, hating the freezing wet sting
of the December downpour, willing the last bus to Trimsaran to
    appear,
fearing his angry words should she be late.
Her shoes let in water,
her one-life plastic bag starts to give way under the
heavy weight of the Christmas presents,
the Asda quarter-pounders
of processed chicken carcass and Simply Value cards.
Her heart sinks. The bus is coming.

Two monstrous eyes light up the sticky wet road, the mean green
    carriage
slowly stops just for her. Only her.
Lonely Llinos climbs aboard, unable to afford the whole
fare home.
She pays until Caegrawn Farm, will walk from there;
avoids the searching stare
of the driver. He knows, it shows.
The pity in his eyes comes from his soul. He won't stop, he'll
    carry on
to her desired destination. To his intense frustration
she avoids his glance.
Just one look would do; imagine the last dance
with this waif of the night, his arms around her fragile form, making
her safe,
protecting, connecting with her frightened mind.

She sits and sighs. Looks out through the filthy window into the
 dirty, black night.

Watching the comfortable world all warm and bright.
Yellow windows with fairy lights
deny her access, leave her guessing at the happiness
within.
Leaving the semi's behind, the steep climb to the woods snakes up
            and up...
into the dark and serious trees, no light to relieve
the sinister gloom; the bus begins to weave
its serpentine way around the treacherous bends;
like a white beacon of hope, the Tafarn y Coed shines pale
in the mist of the moody night.

But Llinos journeys on, mind on the evening to come,
the work to be done, Attila the Hun and his shotgun
behind the pantry door.
Just for rabbits, that's all. Her mind closes down, she's not home yet.
Her Oxfam coat is warm enough, a five pound bargain in hot fuschia,
            but her thoughts are as
cold as the bleak countryside.
In the driver's mirror, her small white face stares heart-shaped back.
            So sad.
He wants her so much, wishes to drive non-stop to the Rock,
 back to Mynyddygarreg, and carry her into his big, white bed
and soothe her sadness away.
What would she say, he wonders....

Her fingers twitch and she picks at the scab on her wrist,
 remembering his fist
from this morning,
 his forced kiss, and the realisation dawning
that nothing will change.
The bus passes the farm, does not stop; calmly she sits and waits.
Waits and dreads the moment of arrival.
The hazy lights of the village draw closer, hostile and mocking.
Her dark eyes close, just for a moment, cancelling all thought,
        blocking the terror
of the angry man in the blue-doored council house, on the forgotten
        estate where
no-one talks anymore....

The knot inside her tightens, she is frightened,
for tonight he may kill her.

MELISSA FU

Then was our eden

There we discovered
the taste of new fruit,
drank deep draughts of air,
wore living bodies,

saw who we could be,
if only we dared
claim the names
already our own.

We had to leave
the garden.

Outside,

as riptides polish
seaglass to pebbles,
you sink deep into my
blood and walking bones.

This love grows.
It grows mute.
Like sky and mountain
It becomes what I know.

Enlighten

A thread that, caught
on some rock or twig,
unravels as you climb.

A lightening, a layer
unweaving, leaving
strands for crows,

filaments strewn
like cobwebs
limned with dew.

At the peak, nothing
shields your shoulders.
Harsh winds, sun

direct on your skin.
Uncovered, exposed,
start here.

SANJEEV SETHI

Argy- Bargies

Singalong of our union had choruses neither you nor I had orchestrated. Its rhythm underscored feelings borrowed from diptych of desire, known to us but not ours. Out of the biorhythm of our conversation was born the need to distance oneself from tremors of togetherness. One was hungry for happy words, unlike *FB* listings as index of happiness.

Godspeed

When emotions are deadweight
they must be discarded. What
are you lugging? A sheath of
shame? March on, guilt-free
soothed in surmise he died
a few years before he actually
did. No need to be apologetic,
no need for, "let's walk away
from each other so they don't
nail us". Let the lobby of life
not stall you: in release is relief.

MARTIN MALONE

War And The Farmer

i.m. Major James Keith of Pitmedden, Aberdeenshire

When it comes to war,
your farmer's a useful sort
and I have had no other hobby.
Each acre has to pull its weight,
the supply of heroes maintained,
and heroes, in turn, must be fed,
ergo three-seventh in oats,
one-seventh in roots
and grass for the other three;
meat, milk, potatoes and bread
cake with bran for the dairy,
and cattle, not sheep, mainly cattle.
                In my life,
I am little heroic
but do, always, what's needed
before I'm compelled, so
when each man has to pull his weight,
I go out with the earliest outgo –
howitzer, limber and six-horse team,
Festubert, Passchendaele, the ridge at Messines,
clear guidance at home for my grieve:
three-seventh in oats,
one-seventh in roots
and grass for the other three;
meat, milk, potatoes and bread
plentiful bran for the dairy,
close, darkening lanes,
our hushed-up wrongs
and cattle, not sheep,
always cattle.

The 1ˢᵗ Women's Battalion of Death

At Bochkareva's petition, Karensky signs off
on the Women's Battalion of Death.
Loath and weary of war but quick enough
to grab a peasant's tit, it's a last ditch bid
to shame broken men back into battle.
Sent up the line near Smorgon, ordered over
the top, lads dither while the girls leave them
behind, pushing on to the German trench
where women well used to drunken fists,
break the trove of vodka before their men
can uncork. This is not fit work for farm girls
and maids who block the path to our retreat.

Like tossing hay onto a cart, that big lass
with her bayonet tears the guts from a Saxon,
and suddenly formations muster everywhere:
1st Petrograd, 2nd Moscow, the Kuban Women's
Shock Brigade yet others without sanction,
charging into action like a new world order
where we don't matter. Of course, you know
what will happen when the lads take a drink.
Karensky won't save them nor will renown,
their medals and good conduct mean little
to drunks and the Tsar will soon be gone.
So, if the boys want fight, you better let them.

NOTE: This was the first women's combat battalion to be organised in Russia just after the abdication of the Tsar in 1917, following a petition by the three times decorated Maria Bochkareva to the Minister of War Alexander Karensky. Despite their bravery in battle - often outstripping the efforts of their male comrades - the women's battalions faced indifference from the authorities and open hostility from many of the men. Bochkareva herself was executed by the Bolsheviks in 1920.

MIMI KHALVATI

Villajoyosa

So that a fisherman far out at sea
returning home as the sun sank or rose,
battling fog and poor visibility
could see, rowing toward Villajoyosa,

among the seafront houses on the shore,
his own abode and by it steer his course,
each house was painted a distinctive colour:
green, ochre, terracotta, pale blue, turquoise.

Of all the blossoms that are out in May,
the lilac – Persian lilac – shares the same
lodestar quality. Never to belong

back in the wild again but to a doorway
where a stranger might hear 'death's outlet song',
it holds the past, only the past in the doorframe.

CHEN CHEN

Interrupted by a Crow: a Syracuse Notebook

Euclid's a catwalk:
frat bro tank tops, grad student
v-necks, blazing leaves

Sex in the shower
interrupted by a crow's
feud with a neighbor

Just the front scraped clean—
our after-blizzard car wears
a mullet of snow

Your cock on my cock
you Upstate boy tall lean hard
hard hard then holy

Again the rain wins
employee of the month, in
the office of mud

Old in overalls,
a man greets small blooms outside
the YMCA

You goop anti-itch
all over the swollen bite
on my face: real love

At the state fair, hens
dyed hot pink—have I ever
looked that fabulous?

Drama queen summer
exits the stage by setting
the trees on fire

BRIAN PATTEN

Talking to Eileen Carney Hulme

One of the things I'm really conscious of in starting this magazine, is that I'm not a poet. I love poetry, but I don't write it and more to the point I'm no Patricia Oxley either. Not that I believe it is all that important, but I have felt that poets talking to poets find another level than that which I inhabit and so I thought it would be interesting to try and arrange things so that at least one of the interviews we have in each issue of 'Arfur' is conducted by a poet rather than by myself. So I am more than pleased to be able to say that in this first issue we somehow managed to coerce two of my favourite poets into an interview, and I was delighted when Eileen Carney Hulme agreed to interview Brian Patten on our behalf.

Here is how it went, with Eileen asking the questions.

MD

Can you remember the first poem that influenced and inspired you?

"I can't remember any one particular poem- none from before I was 12, but there were paragraphs and images from poetic stories like Rip van Winkle and various wordy comics that must have taken root. The comics were intensely colourful pull-outs from the pages of USA newspapers. They were collected by seamen doing the Atlantic crossings from Liverpool to America and were passed on to us kids when they came home on shore leave. Visually the images and storylines were worlds beyond UK comics like The Beano.

Though there were no poems around there were special words and phrases that I picked up on. I'm thinking of words like 'petrified'. A petrified kingdom was more fascinating than a lost one, just as a petrified forest was more full of strange wonders. (Though any forest seemed magic living in the back streets of Liverpool amongst the debris of the Luftwaffe.)

Stories like the tale of Rip van Winkle might have led me towards becoming a writer, but becoming a poet? I don't know. That needs something else to have been triggered along with the desire to write. Something needs to have triggered a deepening of empathy. I grew up amongst damaged people and maybe watching the adults as a child and seeing their vulnerabilities and unhappiness could have had something to do with me becoming a poet."

You were only 21 when Little Johnny's Confession was published and in the same year The Mersey Sound with Adrian Henri and Roger McGough. What do you remember about that time and the putting together of both collections?

"The gestation of a book took longer back then. From putting a manuscript together to the finished book could have taken a year, that's how long many publishers worked ahead, so I'd have been twenty when those two books were first suggested, and I'd have been sitting in an attic with a broken skylight trawling through lots of rough drafts and juvenilia written over the previous three or four years to find enough poems to make a book. Though there were a few obvious poems - like Little Johnny's Confession, that I'd put in a magazine I edited at the time called underdog. (I started underdog when I was 16 or 17. Many of the poems by Roger, Adrian and myself that ended up in The Mersey Sound first saw the light of day in the magazine.)"

You have read with such poets as Neruda, Ginsberg and Stevie Smith. How did it feel to read with those poets and do you have any particular memories to share?

"In 1972 I'd been the token young poet reading with Stephen Spender, Adrian Mitchell and Pablo Neruda at London's Festival Hall. Neruda was considered the century's greatest poet and I grew up loving his work, but I found Stevie far more fascinating, she read in such a weird and wonderful way. Still, Robert Graves was the real poet-hero of my youth. He lived apart from the literati and other poets of the day on Mallorca, in Deia, back when many of the roads were unpaved, doors were always open and wine was cheap. I first saw him walking down a track beside an olive grove. He was tall, wild haired and carried a basket of figs he'd just gathered. He was with the painter Paul Hogarth who I knew vaguely. They were on their way to a bar and invited me to join them. Graves was fascinating. He's known Lawrence of Arabia and even been to tea with Thomas Hardy. He talked about both, as well as about magic rings and brass bands."

Alongside your poetry for adults you have also written many books for children. What was the inspiration behind writing for children and is one more enjoyable than the other?

"There's a lot of playing with words and anarchy in children's verse, and writing poems for children is great fun. I like the way rhyme can lead the poem in different, unexpected, directions."

Do you have a writing routine?

"No, I never have. If I'm feeling enthusiastic about something I'll do it. But basically I'm lazy. A writing routine implies having a "job", which I haven't had since I gave up being a cub-reporter on a local newspaper when I was 18."

Can you say a little about your editing processes and when you decide a poem is complete?

"A handful of poems have written themselves and remain unaltered- they seem to have been born whole and come as gifts. But otherwise I make lots of drafts- at least three-quarters of a poem will be different in varying degrees to the first draft. More and more often now writing a poem is not only trying to find a new or right way (for me) to say something, but also to understand something. Sometimes I'll give up on a poem and put it aside for months, other times I'll scrap it. As for completing a poem, I think it was Auden who said a poem is never finished, only abandoned."

Of your poetry collections for adults is there one book that in some way means more to you than the others and if so, why?

"The Collected Love Poems, because they're the most intense."

I believe you have been working on a memoir, how is it that coming along and what else are you working on at the moment?

"I keep putting the memoir aside because it's a bit absurd someone who is basically private bothering to write a memoir in the first place. As for what I'm working on at the moment, I've gone back to writing rhymes. Recently, I was over in Morocco where I've spent the last few winters renting a house. A very sweet sufi family of drummers owned a marvellous riad next door, and I started writing some sufi inspired verses. I'm probably calling the collection *The Book of Upside-Down Thinking*. There's a donkey in it. I don't mention the donkey's name in the collection, but it's name's Ego. *The Book of Upside Down Thinking* is basically fun, and it's being published by some friends who have a little company that publish gift books mainly. So it might end up in gift shops and not bookshops- we'll see. No harm in that.

I keep on meaning to get round to putting together a more serious book, a collection of elegies – so many friends have gone - but I'm pretty out of touch with publishing these days, and as I said, I'm lazy."

You can find out more about Brian at his web site,

www.brianpatten.co.uk

whilst Eileen's web site is at,

www.freewebs.com/eileencarneyhulme/index.htm

ALISON LOCK

Revealing the Odour of Earth

Sitting down to read Alison Lock's collection *Revealing the Odour of Earth* for the first time, I couldn't help but notice what a beautiful pamphlet her publisher, Calder Valley Poetry have produced. I don't mind admitting that I'm quite in love with the detail when it comes to such things, and the quality of the work is very high by any standard, providing a substantial platform for what is a quite exceptional collection of poetry.

And exceptional it is as Alison is that classic poet/observer to whom no detail goes unnoticed, with an eye for the tiny quirks that in many ways make this country so beautiful. It is very much a collection with a sense of place and time, as Alison gently brings your attention to the land she is hyperaware of, and then widens your gaze to see so much more than what is in front of your nose.

That is what is really important, for me about this collection, as whilst you could easily fall into the trap of thinking it is a cottage garden of a book, scratch the lichen away and there is so much more to find.

I asked Alison a few questions about the collection,

You open your collection with 'November 9th 2016', a poem placing you on the day Trump won the election. It is almost a JFK kind of thing, 'Where were you when...' Do you think poetry has a responsibility to address politics?

"I believe that poetry is mostly a personal expression of the poet's inner world, but naturally, the outer world affects the personal in many ways. I don't believe that the individual has a responsibility to address politics, but if they are motivated to do so, then it will become part of their authentic artistic output. Writing out of a sense of responsibility might reduce their creativity.

Last year, news of the US election campaign flew across the ocean in a relentless daily cacophony. Here, the final count coincided with a falling of snow, and we woke up to a world that was different from the previous day. This seemed to me to be of great significance, and indeed, auspicious. I felt that more than ever this was a time when the natural environment was a place to go to, not only for solace, but to gather thoughts, to meditate, and perhaps to gain some knowledge from the natural environment."

A lot of your poetry revels in the detail of nature. There is a real joy to your writing, how does it make you feel when you read it back?

"When I read my poems, it takes me back to that day/time/place: the moment of inspiration. It doesn't take much for me to be off down a tunnel of memory and imagination. Capturing these moments has become important to me as life passes along its way and I now have an Instagram account dedicated to things that catch my eye, so I will not forget them. Sometimes these images will end up in a poem. "

I love the fact that you are willing to experiment. What attracted you to Simon Zonenblick's form for your poem 'Octolune?'

"Using form in poetry is a way of further expressing an idea; it encapsulates the words, giving them another dimension. When I write, I don't generally start with the idea of a form, but I liked the simplicity of Simon's Octolune. On this occasion, I found the form - an eight-line poem addressed to or about the moon - to have a grounding or anchoring effect."

It seems that you must spend as much time watching as writing; are you by nature an observer?

"Like many writers, I'm an observer, and an absorber of the moment - often the scent in my case - I have a good sense of smell!"

More generally, can you tell us about the collection as a whole, what drove you to put it together?

"Most of the poems in this collection were written last year, within a few months, which might be why they seem to form a natural collection. Nevertheless, the poems are not presented in the order they were written; that happened during the process of collation and by allowing the themes to flow one into the other. I'm very pleased that you think they work well as a whole - that is what I had hoped for."

Again generally, can you tell us a little about your influences?

"Whenever I'm asked this question, I feel under pressure to come up with a list of poets and poems, but although I read a lot of poetry and prose I do not feel particularly influenced by one or two writers. Indeed there are too many to mention. I know this sounds evasive, but I write because I feel compelled to write not because I am influenced or wish to emulate another."

Do you like to attend poetry readings, and do you read your own poetry out loud?

"Yes, I enjoy the opportunity of reading in public, but mostly I love to listen to other poets reading their work. I find that every poet is unique (of course they are) but hearing the words spoken by the writer expands the context and contents, and along with the timbre and cadence of the voice, a live reading brings new dimensions to the work. There's nothing else like it!"

What have you planned next?

"My plan for the immediate future is to launch my new collection of short stories – *A Witness of Waxwings*, Cultured Llama Press, December 2017. But I am always writing new poems as I go along..."

>
> Alison Lock
> 'Revealing the Odour of Earth'
> ISBN: 978-1-9997062-3-4
> Publisher: Calder Valley Poetry
> www.caldervalleypoetry.com
>
> Alison's Instagram account can be found at:
> www.instagram.com/momentsofpoems

PENNY RIMBAUD

What Passing Bells

For our younger readers, the name Penny Rimbaud is perhaps one you have come across because of the collaboration with Tim Burgess of the band The Charlatans on *Singing The Body Electric*. For those of us a little longer in the tooth department, we probably grew-up listening to Penny's band Crass as it created some of the most consistently stunning and challenging music of the last fifty years. Not that Penny is a man to hark to the past, and so it was regarding his current work, the recent recording of an album of Wilfred Owen's poetry, 'What Passing Bells,' that I came to talk to Penny.

The album saw Penny working with two fantastic musicians in Liam Noble, (Piano) and Kate Shortt, (Cello) together creating one of the most heart breaking and stunning portrayals of war and the pain running through Owen's words I have ever heard. Owen's poetry is, of course, impossible to ignore, but Rimbaud's performance is like nothing else and with the subtle interactions Shortt and Noble consistently weave it is totally compelling.

It is of course the centenary of both the end of the First World War and Owen's death, but Owen's words are relevant all of the time, not just to be rolled out for an anniversary, and in recording this album, and performing this work, Rimbaud brings something very important back to the centre of the stage, ensuring that it can't be ignored or forgotten, along with all the people who died alongside or on the other 'team' from Owen.

I was delighted to be able to talk to Penny about the album and we're really pleased to be able to reproduce the interview here.

Penny, before we talk about Owen, can you tell us what your earliest inspirations were?

"The earliest was probably Walt Whitman or perhaps Steinbeck and Hemmingway. I always felt that Steinbeck was a Socialist which at the time seemed to be important.

I think I was about 14 when I heard about the Beats, and had an affinity with John Osbourne who was this angry young man whilst Hemmingway was more transcendental. But it was the idea of the Beats that intrigued me even if at that point I really didn't know who or what they were. I remember going into the American Book Shop on Gooch Street, and being (14 after all) embarrassed to ask for this thing 'The Beats' and so spent an age looking around on my own for anything that mentioned them, it or whatever it was. Finally I found this book by Whitman with a photograph of him on the cover with a fedora and a beard – surely that made him a 'Beat?' – and so I bought that and scurried out of the shop and to the station. On the train home I was transfixed, this was like nothing else I had ever read. He may not have been a Beat, but he was radical and revolutionary and that was amazing in its own right. It was only later that I found out that Whitman had inspired the Beats, so I suppose I got there via my own route in the end, by happy accident."

Did Whitman stay with you?

"Oh yes, I fell in love with his grandeur. He had this democracy of love, not any kind of faux political democracy. I still read and love his work now, he really did become a lifelong friend."

Can I ask what inspired you to record a selection of William Owen's Poetry?

"In many ways it goes back to the very start. I was born during the war and it wasn't until I was three or four that I met my Father. Like many children, I didn't know who he was when he came back after the war and I didn't like him very much. I didn't really know what war was and he didn't want to talk about it. All that I remember him talking about was what he called the 'Real World' which to me sounded a horrible place. This was reinforced later when I discovered a book about Auschwitz among my Mother and Father's books, with all these horrendous images. I got more and more convinced that I didn't fancy this 'Real World' and that I would do anything I could to avoid it. In fact at home all I was able to do was listen to Brahms, it was the only music my Father had. I grew to love Brahms, but not as much as I liked Benjamin Britten. As I got older, I was a chorister and sang in most of the cathedrals in Southern England. I love choral music, although Christianity made no sense to me. Why would you worship...how is a corpse on a cross meant to make you happy?

But it was as a chorister that I very luckily found myself singing as part of the first performance of Britten's 'Spring Symphony.' Britten conducted it himself. He was a lovely man, very involved, compassionate, and this gave me an interest in music that Brahms hadn't. I started to listen to his work, although my Father didn't approve - far too modern for his tastes."

Was this when you discovered the *War Requiem*?

"Very much so, it was the *War Requiem* that was my introduction to Wilfred Owen. I'd still got this hatred of the idea of my Father's 'Real World' and reading a line from Owen, 'I am the enemy you killed, my friend' for the first time it all began to make sense to me.

It resonated far beyond Owen's and mine own self-interest. I didn't immediately understand what it was that made it important, but it gave me a clue and I was at that stage in life when you are searching for clues, trying to make sense of it all. At this point I was very sure what it was I didn't want to be in life, but I was still searching around to find out what it was that I wanted to become. It was all clues I was following and as I reached my 20s it all started to come together. Owen, Britten, I had discovered Zen and was becoming very interested in that, and then there was CND and Aldermaston."

Did the music and your lyrics for Crass grow out of all of this?

"Yes, I had a brief flirtation with Rock 'n' Roll but that was only very short and until I discovered Jazz, and then Jazz was everything, coupled with proper blues - people like Leadbelly rather than the pale, white version that was becoming popular. Once I started playing with bands, I think I always wanted my own version of Owen, but I was never sure how to. In fact the final Crass album contained what I can only describe as this elongated, freeform rant, that was the closest I came to Owen. I remember sending a copy to Peter Pears, Benjamin Britten's musical and personal partner who had sang on the *War Requiem*, along with a note explaining that I was inspired by his and Britten's work. I never heard back, but I hope he liked it."

How did you come to record *What Passing Bells?*

"It started about 10 years ago. I was playing with Liam (Noble, Piano) and Kate (Shortt, Cello) and really wanted Liam to help me set

Owen's poems to music, but it never quite happened, although it was always in the back of my mind as something I should do 'sometime.'

By 2014, I'd become aware that the centenary celebrations were starting to happen, and it was very much a 'now or never' moment. I was really concerned that we would see a lot of jingoism, and hoped that Owen could prove to be an antidote to that. In truth that hasn't happened so far, but regardless I feel as though we have done our bit in putting this out.

But yes, it was in 2014 and myself and Liam were to play the Owen poems at the Vortex Jazz Club in London and by chance I met Kate the day before and invited her along, and she joined us for the second half of what turned out to be the first performance of *What Passing Bells*.

Since then we have played it perhaps half a dozen times. It is an incredibly complex and powerful experience, to play and perform and is immensely draining, but there is a vital, raw energy and power to it. It is of course never the same twice and Kate and Liam create the whole piece anew every time which makes it difficult for me as obviously Owen's words have to be the same, but I need to reinterpret them for the music.

As for how it came to be recorded, I didn't know how it would happen and I was expecting to be trying to find the money to do it, and probably paying for the recording myself, but I was speaking to Derek Birkett at One Little Indian records, who years ago, back in the Punk days I had given a copy of the *War Requiem* to and he had loved it, and he just volunteered to record the album. As simple as that. This was fantastic as it meant that suddenly we could record it in the very best studios with all the best equipment. It turned out to be a fabulous recording - we even got to use Freddy Mercury's piano, which was particularly special."

How did you go about selecting the poems to use?

"I think from the start I was aware that I wanted to make sure that there was a narrative flow, that it worked as a story through the timeframe of the performance, so the performance was really split into two parts and I tailored the poem selection along those lines.

The first half concentrated on the domestic, Owen's life before the War, then moved forward to the training camps, ultimately ending as Owen moved out toward the fight and onto the trains that would take him there.

The second half was to be much broader, to look at the war itself and is ultimately a lot more philosophical as you follow Owen in the full knowledge that by this point he was well aware that the journey he was on, along with all of his friends and mates, could only really end in either death or madness. He would be a mental case or dead, it was as simple as that."

How did this translate into the performance?

"It was very, very passionate and to be totally frank it is a harrowing performance to give. In the end I stopped performing it as two parts, I think it was at King's College London on the Strand that I did it as one piece the first time, and the tiredness of the performance became part of it all. By the end I either burst out in anger or into tears, it is very emotional for me as a performer and for the audience. You see the reaction to it is almost physical."

You differ from Britten by not finishing the piece on *Strange Meeting*, why is that?

"I just didn't feel that I could finish in the same way. Britten's piece was so powerful you had to either choose to try and replicate that power, and it is frankly impossible without being Britten to do that, or you do it your own way, which is how I chose to go.

I decided to finish with *The End* as that seemed to fit perfectly, and it has stayed that way throughout, in all of the performances and now onto the album."

Will there be any more shows?

"Probably not many and there won't be a gig on the date of Owen's death as that could be a little naff, although as it is the centenary year it should really be done properly to finish it all off. As I said, my big concern would be that it would become some sort of right wing jingoistic celebration, but thankfully it doesn't seem to have happened that way so perhaps it allows us to look at Owen and his life, his work with cooler heads. Which is far more fitting."

What is it about Owen that continues to inspire you ahead of the other war poets?

"The interesting thing is that after the wars, Owen was relatively unknown, especially compared to Graves and Sassoon who were the real poster boys, if they can be called that. It wasn't until Britten's *War Requiem* that Owen began to receive any publicity, and then once the Peace Movement and CND adopted him he started to steam forward. This was an incredible time, John Coltrane was recording *A Love Supreme* and the young were starting to flex their muscles. It was a heady and important time and it felt as though the world could change. And Owen, Owen's humanity was a big part of that as he was different to the others. Owen wasn't rich and hadn't been to Oxbridge like Graves, he was poor and from the working class. This gave him a different form of compassion to the other over-educated poets. He had a genuine closeness and feeling for the other men around him and he was never patronising which is always common to all Oxbridge persons."

Did you study Owen in any way?

"I've never been interested in reading biographies, but Owen was different as whilst his poems quite clearly spoke enough, I always felt that there was more to it than it seemed. To me Owen had this almost excruciating tenderness throughout his poetry that indicated a homoerotic level to it all. With this in mind I decided that I would read more about him, to try and understand him more. This is when I found that there were only two meaningful biographies about Owen, one that concentrated on him sexually and the other that didn't. In truth I didn't really care about his sexual persuasion, so I went for the second that avoided it and learned a lot more about the man. It does bother me though, as if Owen was gay it was at a time that he clearly couldn't do anything about it, it was a long time before it became legal after all. Obviously that differs from Britten who was both gay and very much out there about it all. Again that was because he was from a certain class where homosexuality could happen and it would be ignored. Owen, if he was gay, would never have had that advantage and it would have to be repressed, although perhaps there are signs of it in his writing."

Why does Britten resonate so much when you think about Owen?

"I think because there are so many parallels and the differences between them, class, possibly sexuality, are so stark. Britten was highly educated, and his compass was set so that he could take part in homosexual activities without any real fear. He probably got a thrill of being with somebody illegal. He had illegal feelings without fear of any consequences. Owen or anybody from his class could never have done that, it is a different way of thinking. So it is the parallels between them, but I was never somebody who wanted to be known as 'somebody who knows about Owen', so research didn't interest me, but the feeling was there that his words indicated that Owen was gay in thought if not in actions.

And once I realised that, it allowed me to reinterpret the way I was performing them - I could do some of them in an erotic way. The image of a young man being sacrificed,

'Nor antlers through the thickness of his curls' an Adonis speared by a bayonet, I can do that very slowly, almost melting, very precise. In doing the poems, I can see that boy and I'm sure that Owen could too."

Going back to Whitman, were you ever tempted to put any of his work to music?

"Before Crass, I was extremely experimental and at that point, yes, I could well have. The closest I got was the Ices 72 Festival (International Carnival of Electronic Sound) at the Roundhouse in 1972. This was really mirroring the Happenings in the U.S and was very Avant Garde. I recited *Mystic Trumpeter* from the balcony as this big statement and if they could hear it, it was wrong (was the feeling about it all.) I'm not sure what people made of this naked bloke in a top hat. Oddly I was meant to be reciting *Howl* but did that instead as it seemed that was the way it was meant to be."

"What Passing Bells" is available from One Little Indian Records at www.indian.co.uk

PAUL MOSS

Poem I Wish I'd Written

I wish I'd written *Seaside* by Rupert Brooke (1885-1905). Taken from his early poems 1905-1911, it is short and poignant and sustains repeated readings.

Brooke is best known as a War Poet, but in these early years he also wrote beautifully about love and the countryside and the sea. In poems such as *Pine Trees in the Sky - Evening* and *Flight*. *Seaside* is from a time spent living on the English Riviera.

In this poem Brooke uses the sea as a marginal place, a place we can be alone and reflect our concerns, on its ever-changing vista.

He is drawn way from the social life of light, music, dancing and friends by the '...unknown. The old unquiet ocean...' Seeking insights to make that decision, whether to leave the comfort of the familiar and venture into the unknown. 'And all my tides set seaward'.

The seaside is a place I love to go to clear my mind and this poem evokes that feeling. This poem gives us is a different view of a familiar war poet.

MATT DUGGAN

One Million Tiny Cuts

If Alison Lock gently prods you in the direction of her gaze and makes you draw your own conclusions, opening Matt Duggan's *One Million Tiny Cuts* quickly makes you realise that there are many ways to get somebody's attention and sometimes it takes a scream in the face to awaken the most zombie-like among us.

Matt is a poet with a lot to say and a determination that you will hear it, and that is in no way a criticism, for what he has to tell us is often vital.

There is a sense of pain in Matt's work that is perhaps both personal and coming from his observations on society, the world, that goes far beyond an idealistic love of the zeitgeist or protest for its own sake.

The danger of letting anger into poetry is of course that with the noise we lose focus, but Matt is never in danger of crossing that line as despite the laser-focussed vividness of his allusion, he is a shrewd and controlled poet that leaves metaphoric time-bombs set to explode in the back of your mind long after reading his work. He is very much an international poet in his technical style and has a jackdaw's eye that seems to find new approaches, new ways to say what I'm sure he feels should be obvious to the rest of us, but clearly isn't far too often.

This is a stunning collection of poetry and one that I have kept coming back to over the last few weeks.

I was pleased to be able to catch-up with Matt and ask a few questions about it all,

Can you tell us what brought you to put this collection together?

"I wanted to put a collection together that not only tackled current contemporary themes but also indulged in the imaginative realms of the mind, where some of the poems deal with what's happening around the world, but also taking in the joys and experiences of travel and myth. And what it's like to live in a modern society today."

It is an incredibly vivid and in a lot of ways angry work - I would imagine the poem selection and order was important, can you talk us through your thinking?

"The order in this collection is very important, I wanted the reader to feel the anger of the poet as well as the pleasures and difficulties we face, I believe that anger can be used for good purposes to underline the current unbalances we face every day. It did take me quite a while to decide on the current order in this collection, as I wanted to thrill yet make the reader think, instead of each poem being much of the same."

Your poetry always seems to have an element of the zeitgeist about it. It interests me to know whether you worry about them being 'dated' - talk of Emojis and Europe - or are the deeper themes always going to resonate, do you think?

"That's a very good question, I don't think they will ever be dated as people will remember Brexit and the day it happened no matter what side you voted for, and with the mentions of modern communication told with a little tongue in cheek, I do think that people that have read OMTC will remember, with texting to Facebook and how we carry on our lives through a screen, I wouldn't say I was a neo-luddite but it certainly has its negative impacts on communication today."

In many ways you remind me of a commentator - a City Lights type of, 'American' poet, but with elements of a layered, more traditional English or European one - how do you blend that use of clarity in terms of language, and layered metaphor and allusion, without sending yourself mad?

"Thank you, I've been influenced by many American poets and English poets, and blending the image and language into a poem can take months, I suppose it is a little mad as I write one line that I will use for a poem I've not written, and if the line fits then the poem seems to build and flow. We all need a little madness from time to time."

Can you tell us a little more about a few of the poems in the collection that particularly caught me,

Empty Rooms

"This was written after observing many empty apartments and so many people scared yet wanting conversation I suppose it goes back to my point about communication today, I wanted to highlight the lonely and not just the elderly but also the young."

The Spaces Left Bare

"This poem was written in Barcelona after stumbling across a protest from locals against rich tourists buying up apartments and leaving them empty for months at a time."

The Echo Chamber

"This is about a neighbour I listened to night after night who was obviously going through some troubles of his own, and having worked in Mental Health for many years, I did end up helping the poor chap out."

> Matt Duggan
> 'A Million Tiny Cuts'
> Publisher: Clare Songbirds Publishing
> www.claresongbirdspub.com

PATRICIA OXLEY

Acumen

When you have an ambition to start a poetry, a literary magazine, you have to begin somewhere. Obviously, you bring your ideas, but we are all standing on the shoulders of our betters and in truth what you think of as a poetry magazine is pretty much defined by what others have done before.

I've said too often that the first poetry magazines I saw were *Acumen* and then *Agenda* and in their different ways they pretty much set the standard for me. They impressed me so much I later even moved on to the 'Bs.' Not that now I've finally gotten around to starting my own magazine that I want to recreate them (I never could in aeons – I think every magazine has its editor's DNA woven in the pages) but they both in different ways informed the way I see poetry and that is something that is with you every day.

All of which nonsense brings me to something far more interesting and it is quite the thrill that Patricia Oxley, legendary editor of *Acumen*, agreed to do an interview for us, although it astonished me that it is the first (other than for the *Acumen* web site) that she has been asked to do, and so I'm doubly honoured to ask Patricia a few questions.

May I ask how you came to edit *Acumen*?

"I was born in Rochdale during the war. Once that ended I moved with my parents to Barrow-in-Furness for around four years then returned to Manchester. My father was a master printer who worked on the Manchester Guardian. I stress 'Manchester' as that paper was very different from the Guardian of today; a paper then known for its correct spelling and use of English, its literary articles and comments by well-known writers of the day who actually knew how to use the language. He told me that though he couldn't help with my homework – I was at grammar school by then – he could at least see to it that my homework was well presented. He taught me many rules culled from his typography learnt as a typesetter for the MG.

I took science subjects at A-level, but never lost that early love of poetry and literature. I met William while doing O-levels and he was very much into the classics at that time so encouraged me to read Homer, Plato, Herodotus etc. And he introduced me to Milton well before school did. And we also read the great novels of the nineteenth century from all over Europe. It was a heady time of discovery for both of us.

Once we married we lived in London for three years where he began to write poetry. Then came family, a move to Epping, career moves for William, being a full-time mother for myself. And all the time, reading, reading. By 1972, William had had his first book published, and, though still at home, I became involved with poetry events and magazines as, like many poets, William tried his hand at editing. The writing became so important in his life that we moved to Brixham. And eight years later, I thought of *Acumen* and you know the rest."

Why did you call it *Acumen*?

"My story, and I'm sticking to it, is that the girls (our two daughters) were in their early teens and didn't rely on mother any more. After rushing around after them for years, I suddenly felt redundant, and bored. It was William who said to me 'Why don't you start a magazine, you know all about that from helping with the ones I used to edit'. I don't know who was most shocked when I answered that I would. Then I needed a name, so we spent over two hours one evening discussing a long list we'd thought up, many names to do with being in the South West. We finally decided on some trivial name or other like South West Review. I felt we'd earned a cup of tea and made for the kitchen saying, 'Now we've decided on *Acumen* we can relax.' We then looked at each other, decided we had heard right so felt we had to go with the name. I always say the magazine named itself."

For you, what makes the magazine so special?

"I think the magazine is very special for when it started there were very few female editors (30 years later it is the exact reverse). Also, and I still think this is almost unique; *I don't write poetry myself.* I am a reader, an appreciator and not a poet.

I started the magazine as I felt that most of the stuff in the little magazines thirty years ago was not fully poetry. It was mainly free verse. Not that I was, or am, against free verse, but in those days 'free' was the operative word with very little 'verse' attached. I started it with a crusading approach determined to bring more poetry to the magazines. Alas, I reckoned without the Poetry Elite. Yes, poetry has changed but in the way the big poetry publishers wanted, changes which reflected the poetry of their published poets. I feel many of the *poems* I publish in *Acumen* are equally as good as the poems they publish, but that often the poets I publish have never been in the right place at the right time; have never studied under one of their poets at

University etc. Also the rise of Creative Writing classes/degrees hasn't helped. Many poets are now professors rather than just writers of poetry and they influence the younger/newer poets so poetry changes but not individually but in a kind of group way.

So where do I see the magazine going? Publishing what I feel is good poetry (sometimes satirical poetry) and helping new writers with a chance to see their best work in print."

Can you remember the first poem that you read that really caught you and made you want to do 'something' involving poetry?
"*Overheard on a Salt Marsh* by Harold Monro. It was acted by two older girls at junior school. I must have been about seven and I fell in love with the language. It felt magical, otherworldly and yet I could feel the rhythm and images within the words.

This was followed by poems like *Sea Fever*, parts of *Goblin Market* (can you imagine that being read to juniors today?), *Cargoes*, Masefield, Wordsworth, *Horses of the Camargue*. So when I started at grammar school I was ready for all the poetry, Shakespeare et al."

When you started the magazine, do you remember what was the first poem that you selected? How exciting was that, to know you'd found something special and that you could share it?

"It was very exciting. The first poem I chose was *The Abandoned* by Dannie Abse. He was the first submitter and the first subscriber to the magazine and I felt honoured that someone like Dannie took an interest in what I was doing."
What is it that you look for in a poem? Do you know a good one when you see it straight away or is there a lot of sifting?

"Any poem which has any kind of appeal – images, word-play, feeling, subject-matter etc – is placed in a short-list. Out of the many poems I read during the four-month period between issues, usually around a hundred to a hundred and thirty find their way into the shortlist. One of the best ways of sorting this shortlist out is to use train journeys to London etc. I carefully read the poems on the outward journey, making a list of those which I think ought to go into the magazine. Then even only 24 hours activity puts all this out of my head. I mix up the poems into a different order, then do the same exercise on the way home. If no journey is available, I try to do the same exercise on either side of a weekend. Then I compare the lists. Those in both lists are 'in' (for the time being), those in neither are 'out' (for the time being). Then I go through the same exercise again with the poems which were only in one list. So it goes on until I have approximately the correct number for the issue. Then, to make sure, I read the rejected poems once again just in case one has worked on me subconsciously (which sometimes happens) and finally read the accepted poems as a batch to make sure they are all of a good standard. This takes around a week to complete."

The Arts Council obviously have reduced their support for poetry in recent years, how important do you think they are now to magazines and by extension to the poets trying to develop their work?

"As it seems only poets read poetry the Arts Council is enormously important. It is like a closed shop where the practitioners write for other practitioners and they form cliques and cross-border – sorry – cross-magazine friendships. Some poets are even known by magazines they are published in, such as 'So-and-so is an *Agenda/Acumen/Orbis* poet. For any magazine to have a decent life and a decent publication, it has to have either private money or an ACE grant."

Your magazine is quite beautifully produced. How important are the 'production values' to you?

"The feel of the magazine as a thing in itself is very important to me. As you saw above I got the love of typesetting from my father and I wish that I could do more on the production front with better paper and thicker covers, I love the cover designs too, some have been really fantastic. I have redesigned the inside a couple of times in the magazine's life, but I like the one I have at the moment. It's quite clear in format and doesn't have too small margins while not making too much white space. If I had more money to spend on production costs (as well as postage and paying poets a miserable pittance) some of these factors might be changed again."

For poets thinking of submitting, what advice do you have for them and what are the errors people make that annoy you?
"The advice is spelt out on the website under journal/submissions.

What annoys me?

Being addressed 'Dear Sir' (not even Sir or Madam), If someone is too lazy to find out the name of the editor, or even to resort to 'Dear Editor', then I am often tempted to be too lazy to read their poems.

Not putting their name and address on each poem (as asked for in the guidelines).

I say on the website that if the poem is rejected, please don't re-submit for at least one month. So when a poet immediately sends in another batch ...

Asking for advice about their poems, then telling me I don't know what I'm talking about if I don't say that the poems are wonderful. This is usually from men!

Being sent poems which are openly sexist and often about rape and the fantasies which men would like to carry out. I feel this is because

I am a woman editor. They get the usual bland rejection letter as I don't want to give them the satisfaction of riling me."

What do you think is the role of the editor?
"To edit. To read all the poems which arrive through the post or in the inbox as soon as possible and return the no-hopers, or even the just-missed-out with a polite note. Not to sit on a submission for up to six months without telling the poet this might happen. If a good poem arrives but I feel a small alteration would help, I tell the poet than leave it up to them whether they make that alteration. 99% usually do, the other 1% again tell me I don't know what I'm talking about."

Reviews are an important way for poets to spread the word about their work, what is *Acumen's* policy?

"I have a reviews editor, Glyn Pursglove, who sends out books for review. Our agreed policy is to have a balance of books from the 'big' poetry presses which publish the more well-known poets and poets from the independent presses. Sometimes he will review a self-published book. I used to worry about a balance of male/female but decided that over several issues this seems to equal itself out. The actual choice of the books reviewed I then leave to him."

In recent years the pamphlet has had quite a renaissance – like vinyl and cassettes for music. Do you like them and given that 'perfect binding' is relatively cheap and easily available is there really still a place for the humble staple?

"The pamphlet is a good starting point for new poets. *Acumen* runs its own series of Occasional Pamphlets. These are for good poets who haven't had a full collection. Something they can take to readings, offer as examples to publishers when soliciting a collection etc. They are also useful for publishing a new kind of poetry or a longer poem by someone who is more well known."

Magazines almost seem to need to create their own 'tribe' of supporters to survive, do you think this is healthy, or do we end-up preaching to the converted?

"It happens, and its not healthy. *Acumen* tries to include many new names with each issue, but this can also back-fire as readers do want to read poems by the more popular poets. A mixture of the two with a leavening of a couple of 'biggish' names seems to be the best mix."

What do you think of the (increasing) number of festivals and competitions – are they a positive thing for poetry? What drove you to start the Torbay Festival?

"The Festival wasn't initiated solely by myself. William and I co-started it when he was Poet-in-Residence for Torbay for the Millennium Year of the Artist celebrations. He had a little ACE funding and we ran the first competition to help out financially. After it was all over, William was glad to get back to writing poetry but I saw that the Festival had been a fun event, full of poetry and friendship (well it had to be friends whose arms we twisted to come and read in Torbay for the small fees we could afford then!). But I felt that it could be an opportunity to give poets a voice and an audience; and to give an audience a taste of good poetry. As with *Acumen*, I wanted to mix recognised poets with others not so well known but who wrote good poetry. So I began building the Festival along those lines. One of the early visitors to the Festival wrote that coming to Torbay was like attending 'one long poetry party'. This seemed exactly right for Torbay; the audiences seem like guests at a party; a party where everyone matters, not just the performers. So the character of the Festival, which grew organically, was formed.

As to running the Festival: there is a small 'permanent committee', as it were, of six people in the Bay. We meet regularly and they are a great help when I need to pass ideas in front of them. They also come up with ideas, comments and criticism. And they are the permanent workers taking several organisational tasks off my shoulders. However, we do have four additional out-of-town committee members who bring a different dimension to the committee, showing us how we are perceived by the non-provincial, wider world.

The increasing number of Festivals and competitions is splitting the audience. With competitions especially, the number of poems entered as a totality over a given area is probably well up. But in the South-West alone (South of Bristol and West of Dorchester) there were only two competitions in 2000 when I started thinking about the Festival and having a competition. Two weeks ago I counted from memory the number of competitions in that area and came up with fourteen off the top of my head. Money is in short supply and people cannot afford to enter too many competitions, so they split their chances by sending one or two poems to more competitions. Most organisers I speak to these days say the numbers are well down on ten years ago.

This will though, in the end, finally become counter-productive. As the profit from the competitions go down, many organisers will begin to think that the work in running a competition isn't worth it, and that competition will cease. And quite often the Festival that it supports financially – especially if it gets no ACE support will inevitably be in difficulty."

Can song lyrics, rap and the rest be seen as poetry?

"Perhaps, but not when the singer repeats the same phrase eighteen times in succession! My teenage grandson calls rap 'failed poetry'."

Has the number of poets who work in academia and who do writing courses, made poetry more technical, sterile and soulless or have you seen an improvement in the abilities of poets?

"Poetry is now, on the whole, better written than it was when I started over thirty years ago. But in one way this makes the genuine article sometimes harder to distinguish from the well written poem which employs a good use of language in a technical way but which, when looked very closely is, as you say, sterile and soulless. All surface meaning and no depth."

What next for *Acumen*?

"To keep it going, to still ask awkward questions of its readers (what good is a long poem? Are translations important? Is being able to read your poetry well part of the creative process?). To be open to all poems if they are good enough. To still enjoy poetry within the magazine."

You can find out more about Acumen at:

www.acumen-poetry.co.uk

CHARLOTTE BEGG

Eye Flash Poetry

As I was completing the interview with Patricia Oxley and noticing that Acumen had reached its 90th edition, I came across a new magazine that was about to launch its first, something which interested me somewhat, as you can probably imagine. As with *Acumen*, the first issue of *Eye Flash Poetry* is utterly unique and quite beautifully proportioned. Produced in pamphlet form it is a total delight (if like me you enjoy fine papers and beautiful art – the unlaminated cover adorned with artwork from the very talented Kitty Cooper definitely hits the mark.)

The poetry inside is far from shabby too, with Joanna Nissel's magazine opener, *Perfect Happiness*, being beautifully quirky, pulling at the threads of forgotten memories. I also have to mention Neil Richards' *The Flood* which caught me with its line about Noah 'Discreetly sewing souls into ants', as did Jim Zola's *Dusk* opening with, 'You become home to your wife's sadness...' which resonates horribly.

But then every poem in the magazine captured my imagination in one way or another and it is a tribute to both editor Charlotte Begg's eye for a good poem and her ability to sequence them through the magazine so that you feel as though you have travelled somewhere, that is most impressive.

As is my want (and clearly needing all of the tips I can get) I was pleased to be able to ask Charlotte a few questions.

Hello Charlotte, can you tell us how you came to edit EFP?

"I have been a long-time collector of small poetry pamphlets and journals but felt there was something missing. I wanted to produce a poetry journal with a strong identity, quirky and unpredictable. Our second issue, being guest edited by the talented Anna Saunders, will have a completely different feel to issue one."

Your first issue is beautiful, how did you decide upon the design?

"Thank you! We worked so hard on all the details of our first issue, I have a super talented partner who created a great layout for the journal, and having Kitty Cooper for the cover art was great- the piece really reflects the poetry collection."

What makes the magazine special? Why did you start it and where do you see it going next?

"I think the energy and passion getting put through *Eye Flash* is amazing- we are so humbled by all the support we have had so far, and the great contributions that keep being sent in. As far as where we are going next- we hope to keep gathering momentum and be able to showcase more poetry and art that will blow our readers away."

Can you remember the first poem that you read that really caught you and made you want to do 'something' involving poetry?

"Oh yes. *Ariel* by Sylvia Plath. I had to stop after the first stanza and compose myself. It took me two more weeks to read it- I just wanted to savour every word. An experience I'll never forget."

When you started the magazine, do you remember what was the first poem that you selected?

"Joanna Nissel's *Perfect Happiness* was one of the first submissions. I remember getting *that* feeling- the feeling when a poem enters you and changes you in a subtle way. Fantastic short poem that packed a punch."

How do you recognise one of those special poems?

"Usually it's quick. The same way a certain glance or grin from someone can wash emotion over you- the same is true for a poem. There have been occasions where the poem grows and ends in such a way it takes my breath away. Both are powerful."

Your magazine is quite beautifully produced. How important are the 'production values' to you?

"Very. The least we can do is present the fantastic poetry in a way that is pleasing to read."

What do you think is the role of the editor?

"To ensure the poetry selected will impact the reader. The selection process is time consuming and requires a certain amount of confidence- the reader should know by which editor has curated the poetry that they are in for a ride! Of course proof reading is part of being editor which again is time consuming, but most of all the role of the editor I believe is to promote the poetry and poets they strongly feel are talented and have something unique to show or tell."

Why do you think that the pamphlet has made such a 'come back' in recent years?

"Individually created collections of music, art, literature and poetry will always hold a special place in people's hearts."

How do you feel about magazines/publishers almost creating their own tribes?

"I think any publication of the creative kind should only preach inclusion."

How do you feel about the number of festivals and competitions that are available to poets?

"The more the merrier I think, but it does make it a bit more of a task to poets to sift through where to the best place to send their work is."

Do you think poetry can be taught?

"The number of courses and information about writing poetry hopefully helps to include and educate poets that otherwise would not gain an insight into the technical process of writing a poem, and I think that is always a good thing. When a poem puts technique before subject then its obvious to the reader."

What next for your magazine?

"We will keep moving forward, gathering more talented poets and artists, and hopefully grow a community that supports one and other."

The second issue of Eye Flash Poetry is about to be released, edited by Anna Saunders.

Find out more at www.eyeflashpoetry.co.uk

PENNY RIMBAUD

America and How!

One of a series of books we have in for review from the quite brilliant Bracketpress, is a collection of Penny Rimbaud's poems that concentrated upon America. All of the poems were written between 1973 and 2012 and as a book it is fascinating to see the degradation of a country through Penny's eyes – from the taste of the life black America was experiencing as he travelled as a 'Hippy in a VW van' across the country and the ministrations that brought from the local police, to the 'military-industrial-nationalist complex solidified into a repressive police bureaucracy' that Ginsberg had predicted but somehow failed to notice was already suffocating him.

It is the response that Penny wrote to Ginsberg's 'Howl' that forms the centrepiece to the book, taking the original as a template and if not 'bringing it up to date', as though it needed it, perhaps reclaiming it and using the distilled message it offered to a new and unknowing audience.

I asked Penny how he came to write the response to *Howl*,

"Eve [Libertine, singer from the band Crass] and I were due to be performing it at the London Jazz Festival. Eve was going to concentrate on Kerouac – the first half of the show would be given over to that, and then I would recite Ginsberg's *Howl* as the second part of the show. It was going to be recorded at the Vortex.'

So what changed?

"As it was to be recorded, of course we had to arrange for the licensing of the poem, and it took a little research as over the years publishing companies had been bought and sold and so had the rights. It surprised me to find that it wasn't City Lights who retained the copyright, but instead it seemed to be that it was owned by Rupert Murdoch, or rather he owned News International who owned Harper Collins and so on. I mean, what kind of madness is that? It is Murdoch's military-industrial-nationalist wing, a total violation of all of the creative ideals I hold dear and somehow they had co-opted *Howl*. I honestly knew that I couldn't read it and so with five days until the performance and the recording I decided I would write my own response, which became *How!*

How did you go about it?

"In many ways, Murdoch gave me the model – his love of the opiate of capital – and so I decided to follow the same structure and metre, to do three parts and then expand on it. Surprisingly, it turned out to be almost identical in line length and whilst it would be pretentious to say that I channelled Ginsberg, it was very easy to write, easy to do and there was some fun in including a hint of 'mid-Atlantic.'"

How was it received?

"Oddly, it is the only time I have ever received a standing ovation, and that was at the Ledbury Poetry Festival of all places. It was really strange in many ways. I had gone with the saxophonist Louise Elliot and turned-up at this school hall. Anyway, there was nobody there and you are thinking 'uh oh' this isn't looking good, and then two punks turned-up who I guess were there because they had heard of Crass and they were obviously feeling out-of-place too. Suddenly the place filled and it was packed within a few minutes by all these blue rinsed ladies drinking champagne.

To be totally honest once we started I expected everybody to walk out and the punks did leave after ten minutes, but the rest of them were silent and just didn't move. It was like Madame Tussauds, you could hardly see anybody breathe even, could of heard a pin drop.

Well, I came to the end and had absolutely given everything, I really was on the point of collapsing and amazingly the people loved it, they went absolutely potty. That was about 15 years ago and I still don't really understand it. I suppose you never know."

Have you performed it since?

"Yes, I did it once at City Lights in San Francisco, no backing just me in front of a big portrait of Ginsberg. I guess the circle turned."

>
> Penny Rimbaud
> 'America and How!
> ISBN: 978-0-9566184-2-9
> Publisher: Bracketpress
> www.bracketpress.co.uk

SANDRA BEASLEY

Count The Waves

In the article we have in the current issue that is planning to follow Sandra Beasley as she creates her next book, she mentions that she thinks in collections. This in many ways sums her up for me in that, like musical artists - singers or bands - have traditionally put albums together, whilst popstars are looking for the quick hit of a quick hit, Sandra very much has a feeling or a sense of togetherness about her work that is perfectly encapsulated within twin covers. Don't get me wrong, I'm sure she can 'slam it' with the best of them, but the continuity of her work across a few dozen pages in her case seems perfect and so it is with *Count The Waves* which for me is almost the perfect collection.

As to why it is different, where to start? Sandra is very much a concept poet, and about half of the poems in *Count The Waves* use an obscure, 19th Century book, A.C Baldwin's *The Traveler's Vade Mecum* as a starting point for her poems.

So many have titles like '*The Traveler's Vade Mecum*, Line #4088: 'In The Latest Fashion' where the original source (I am guessing as Sandra doesn't explain) provides a jump-off point from which her own creativity is ignited. I don't know Baldwin's work, so I'm not entirely sure whether her poems have much to do with the original in any way other than as a spark to her own, but in constructing a mechanism by which she almost automatically prompts herself, she creates a body of work that is in some way thematically linked way before she writes a line.

All of which is interesting and intriguing but absolutely pointless if the poetry created as a result of the concept doesn't do anything worth all of the time, but this of course is where the talent comes to play as Beasley writes vibrant and neon-tinted poetry that is intellectually full of play and emotionally charged with tenderness and love. If it wasn't the easiest way to kill any poet's career you could her easily compare her to Sylvia Plath, but dare I say (without being stoned for it) that there is far more going on with Beasley's poetry than Ms. Plath ever managed and her love of the Sestina is beautiful to behold.

How Sandra follows this, well she says she will be throwing away the template and starting again and if that means an audience lost, so be it. For any other poet you would have to take that with a pinch of the salty stuff, but with her you know that however far she travels from counting the waves, the journey and ultimate destination will no doubt be something special.

    Sandra Beasley
    'Count The Waves'
    ISBN: 978-0-393-35321-1
    Publisher: W. W. Norton
    www.wwnorton.com

S.A. LEAVESLEY

How To Grow Matches

I'm probably a little pre-occupied by the idea of new publishers at the moment for some reason, but one that I have been particularly impressed by is the rather cool Against The Grain Press, put together by Abegail Morley, Karen Dennison and Jessica Mookherjee.

Aiming very high in terms of their attention to detail and the design/production values of the pamphlets they are producing, they haven't forgotten the most important part of all and have already published two quite gifted poets in Anna Kisby, who's collection helped launch the press toward the end of last year and now S.A. Leavesley with her collection, How To Grow Matches.

From the off, I have to say that I am a big fan of S.A Leavesley, finding her work consistently brave and challenging in all the right ways, with a forensic ability to turn all of your preconceptions on their head with a single syllable. There are quite literally no throwaway or wasted words in this collection, with every one of them considered and placed precisely to engender exactly the response, emotionally, intellectually, that the author requires.

This is powerful stuff, but it is Leavesley's ability to use the form of the pamphlet as part of the work that is particularly impressive.

Because there *is* a difference between a book-sized collection and a pamphlet that seems to often be overlooked by poets and publishers alike.

For me a pamphlet can either be used like a novella, where compared to a novel it focusses on a single topic, has a single story to tell, or instead it can be a smaller collection of poems, but where repetition – all of the 'fat' – is carved away and what you are left with is the real 'meat', the genuine source of what the poet has to say without any prelude or development of themes.

It is the latter where Leavesley is the absolute owner of the form, and in *How To Grow Matches* you have a collection of poems that really wouldn't work, would lose a lot of its power, if it simply had another twenty poems bolted-on.

I'm pleased to say that I had the opportunity to ask the author a few questions shortly before we went to print,

The collection works beautifully as a set and flows really nicely, do you think in terms of collections or do you collect your poems?

"Thank you! The short answer is both. My first collection *Into the Yell* (Circaidy Gregory Press) and my fourth *plenty-fish* (Nine Arches Press) came together afterwards – sifting for the best or most popular pieces and then refining from that. My second and third collections *Be[yond]* and *The Magnetic Diaries* (Knives Forks and Spoons Press) had narrative and theme constraints which meant they were written as pamphlet/collections. Likewise with my two earlier pamphlets: *Hearth* (Mother's Milk Books) was a commissioned collaboration with Angela Topping and *Lampshades & Glass Rivers* (Loughborough University), a narrative sequence.

After the publication of my collection *plenty-fish*, I realised my new writing was falling into three fairly distinct subject areas. One of these was poems with strong female voices, characters and concerns. I created a 'draft collection' document with these initial pieces and every time I had a new poem that fitted this, I also copied it into this draft collection.

With *How to Grow Matches*, I ended up with more than enough poems for a full collection but that meant I could filter out any that covered too similar ground or didn't contribute to the pamphlet as a whole work in itself.

I love the potential for focus, cohesion and flow with the pamphlet form. I think putting it together in this way means there's always a small part of the subconscious aware of where an individual piece might fit within the bigger pamphlet-length picture. The ordering certainly felt easier working in this way, though there are always some poems that are harder to place around."

The collection very much nails the times in terms of #metoo etc. but you widen the scope by making a lot of it feel personal - was this a deliberate approach, to take an observers stance?

"The poems, and the pamphlet itself, actually precede #metoo. But issues of gender, sexism, stereotyping, the portrayal of female characters in myths, conflicting potential role models and societal expectations...these have been around since, well, the year dot.

In terms of the personal, I guess I do feel that people's lives are where politics is really seen and felt. Also, that this is where my political beliefs stem from, who I am as a person, how I was brought up, what I've seen and felt.

In terms of the observer stance, I've used the first person a lot in the past, to get close to adopted personas and fictional characters as much as to write about personal experience. But in poetry it can be hard sometimes for readers to know whether to take the first person as the poet's own life or not. With this pamphlet, I consciously wanted to use the second person (ungendered but personal) and third person (gendered but potentially more distanced/observational) and the dynamics between the two. With this, simultaneously not claiming the experiences as my own, yet at the same time maybe a sense that women across time may have similar stories and experiences, even within very different settings and across very different backgrounds."

There seems to be an overlap between imagination, experience and observation across the collection. How easy do you find it to take differing approaches/adopt different perspectives?

"Good question, and not something I'd considered consciously. The fact that I've probably partly answered this in the previous question may be a good indication that overlapping and moving between these is something that just happens when I write. I have eclectic tastes in terms of reading but also my other interests – from walking and photography, to surfing and climbing. I've worked as a newspaper journalist, I write fiction and creative non-fiction, and I turned one of my poetry collections into a play. Hybrid forms, working at genre-boundaries and overlappings of all sorts is something that I really enjoy. Maybe, subconsciously, I'm just trying to twist Emily Dickinson's 'Tell all the truth but tell it slant' to see if there are any slants that aren't possible..."

Can you talk a wee bit about a few of the poems - how you came to write them, influences, inspiration:

a. *Fashion Chains*

b. *The cow that ate all the plums,* and

c. *All the women left*

"I'm going to work backwards with this list, because it's reverse chronology on the writing, so it's easier to remember in that order.

All the women left was written after a visit to Birmingham Symphony Hall, not for a concert, simply passing through the building. At the same time, I was thinking about apocalypses and women-only tribes. The poem title came to me first, wondering what if there were only women left in the world? But I liked that it also had another potential meaning: what if, as a protest, all the women left an event? I don't want to give too much away about the poem's eventual narrative. But essentially, it's a poem imagining the latter happened for a concert. A potential added irony with the scenario is that, if all the women left, half the audience might leave a concert but if all the female musicians left would that only leave half the performers?

The cow that ate all the plums is entirely my dad's fault. My grandparents were farmers on the Gloucestershire-Wales border. My mum and dad slowly converted one of the family barns into a house, where they lived once my sister I left home. The house is surrounded by fields and my dad told me the story about the cow that would eat all the plums, not to get drunk as such but presumably because the cow found the tippsiness quite pleasant. (I was conscious of potential fruit and orchard Garden of Eden connotations or that plums, for example, might make readers think of William Carlos William's *This Is Just To Say* but these are more part of the general incidental background than necessary elements to the poem.) The final images of the poem arose naturally through thinking about slang use of the word 'cow' and similar human scenarios.

Fashion Chains is a three-part sequence influenced both by and against Sylvia Plath. I don't altogether like or easily read some of Plath's work. But I admire the boldness. It's hard to be a female poet, writing about women's life and mental health issues without feeling Plath there, sometimes in a good way but also as a shadow or a yardstick to be measured against and fail.

Saying this isn't to ignore many other important female poets, simply that there are too many to list here, and this poem in particular is influenced by Plath. The first part of the sequence imagines fashion-store shop windows at night – a kind of contemporary version of Plath's *The Munich Mannequins*. The second part moves focus from the plastic models to the shop-window glass and part-reflections – ghost-like but sunlight sheering off too, like a photographer's flash-bulb, perhaps.

Also, for me, an awareness of the fast pace and transient/disposable nature of modern life, and how easy it is to not look carefully and to miss things in not doing so, the surface level potentially becoming all there is. The third part then takes the text of Plath's *The Munich Mannequins* and strips away some of the words. Symbolically what is left might be rain on glass, sunlight glancing off the shop window, the plastic model without its clothes, the bare bones of society, or... I hope that this sequence, like the other poems, will allow for these possibilities but also be open to other interpretations, personal to each individual reader.

    S.A. Leavesley
    'How To Grow Matches
    ISBN: 978-1-9997907-1-4
    Publisher: Against The Grain Press
    againstthegrainpoetrypress.wordpress.com

ISABELLE KENYON

This Is Not A Spectacle

One of the most interesting poets around at the moment is Isabelle Kenyon and if S.A. Leavesley encourages you to look at the fragmented minutiae, Isabelle is definitely asking you to take a step back and look at the full panorama with her broadbrush paintings of the realities of life. Not that there is any lack of subtlety, she is as capable as any of winkling out and displaying the finest of details, but you get the feeling that, in many ways like Matt Duggan's collection, *This is Not a Spectacle* not only had to be written, but it very definitely had to be written NOW.

This is a strong and positive collection of poems, at times personal but never crossing the line into overly sentimental, and it is really one that I think you will want to explore for yourself.

I asked Isabelle about her book,

Why did you feel that you wanted to put the collection together?

"I think my motivation came from wanting to share my voice as a poet for the first time and see what reaction people would have to my social commentary and my experiences!"

Do you think in collections or is it an amalgamation of poems written over a period of time?

"I don't tend to think in collections - but I find that when I do, I am much more productive. For example, I have a chapbook being published later this year by Clare Songbirds Publishing House, New York, which I wrote entirely in New Zealand, about my time there. It was so easily cohesive because my theme was niche."

I love how visual your poetry is. Is that something you have to work at?

"Thank you! I don't actually realise I'm writing in a visual way - but the poetry I love to read is rich in imagery, and I think I'm a bit of a visual thinker myself."

In terms of your influences, you seem to have quite a playful side, who (if anybody) do you feel influenced this?

"I come from a very sarcastic family and we all have a dark sense of humour..."

Having been homeless, your section of poems seem very much to me to hit the mark. Is this an area you researched or have experience of?

"That's really interesting - it feels like an important issue to me. I feel as though it is something swept under the carpet by governments. I have worked briefly with homeless charities while teaching teenagers drama - introducing them to communities they might not otherwise interact with and challenging their stigmas about people who are homeless."

Can you give s some background on how you came to write:

Domestic –

"This one was actually a fridge magnet exercise in a workshop! So it's not personal experience. Fridge magnets inspired me..."

The Man With The Unfortunate Name –

"I feel as though I live on trains at the moment and I overhear so many conversations, I can't help but eavesdrop and be inspired..."

Granny Olga –

"My Granny Olga inspired me to write from a very young age. She was a talented poet and researcher into the history of women's writing, and I like to honour her in my poetry. She forms my identity in many ways. She was also the kind of person who went out onto the streets of Manchester with food she had just cooked to give to the homeless."

> Isabelle Kenyon
> 'This Is Not A Spectacle'
> ISBN: 978-1976074899
> Publisher: Fly On The Wall Poetry
> www.flyonthewallpoetry.co.uk

ISABELLE KENYON

Please Hear What I'm Not Saying

In between creating her collection, *This Is Not A Spectacle* the indefatigable Miss Kenyon has also been editing an anthology of poetry, *Please Hear What I'm Not Saying* in support of the mental health charity Mind.

This, by its nature, is quite a large collection with over 100 poets creating by turn some seriously raw and touching poetry that will shock, horrify and at many points make you cry, not so much at the horror of mental illness, that isn't that unusual, but at the lack of opportunities for treatment that penny-pinching politicians and the people they claim to represent cause on a daily basis.

But as I say, this is a large book and will take a bit-more-reading than I'm afraid I had the opportunity to do before the deadline for this wee review, but suffice to say it has some great work in there from people like the excellent Jane Burn, the rather awesome Angela Topping and so many more it is embarrassing not to be able to name them all, so I will leave it there.

In summary, a really good read and for a fantastic cause, so what is not to like? I asked Isabelle about this too, of course,

How did the idea of the anthology arise?

"I had an open call out for submissions - with a fantastic response. I then selected the poems which I felt would complement each other and offer a wide range of experiences of mental health."

Is Mind something that has a special meaning to you?

"All of my family have experienced mental health problems, more or less, in some way or another. That's normal. But the current help for what is now a norm for 1 in 4 people isn't enough and Mind is a charity which fills this gap."

What do you consider makes the book a success?

"I think this book is successful when it touches the hearts of the readers and when they can relate to it."

Are there any particular poems that mean something to you?

The Sound of Metal by Anna Kander –

"This one is about her brother, who cannot find the words to say the sexual trauma he has suffered, and leaves home and he never comes back.

It terrifies me that males in particular suffer a stigma of reaching out or speaking out for fear of being seen as 'weak'."

Borderline by Hilary Walker –

"Her struggle with her daughter, who suffers from borderline personality disorder. The battle of someone hating you but needing you - your love being spat back in your face...but suffering with mental illness, is the daughter to blame? These questions that can't be answered haunt me too."

Soot by Owen Gallagher –

"The electric shock treatment for 'the crazies' - how did we ever put people through that?"

    Editor,. Isabelle Kenyon
    'Please Hear What I'm Not Saying'
    ISBN: 978-1984006646
    Publisher: Fly On The Wall Poetry
    www.flyonthewallpoetry.co.uk

SANDRA BEASLEY

The Building of a Collection

One of the (far too many) ideas we have had for the magazine, is to follow a poetry collection being 'built' over however long it takes. It is easy enough for us to read a book, or ask some questions once it is all over, but how often do you get to sit in the corner whilst the magic happens?

But we needed a special kind of poet, a special kind of person, who is willing to let us hitch along for the ride, and I am more than pleased to be able to say that when I suggested such a scenario to one of my favourite poets, Sandra Beasley, she didn't call security or otherwise laugh in my face. Instead she said 'why not', and here we are.

The plan is that we will ask Sandra a couple of questions in each issue to see how things are going, and for this our 'opener', we took a few more moments of her time than intended and asked her to set the scene.

Sandra, the big question for me is how you go about following-up a collection like *Counting The Waves*. Where do you start – have you a title in mind or an idea of the number of poems it will contain?

"I prefer working with a title—to be literal, when carrying around a loose stack of pages, though each is still un-numbered, I prefer having a "title page" on top of the stack. So I've been playing with the phrase "How History Claims Us," which is a line from a poem in the collection. On a thematic level, this book is interested in American history, myth-making and memorializing, and my specific experiences growing up in and around DC as the daughter of an Army general. Quite a number of food poems pop up, in part because that's a vivid access point to tradition, and in part because I've been simultaneously working on editing an anthology for the Southern Foodways Alliance. In arranging a book, I'm drawn to symmetry; each of my previous three collections have been divided into three sections, with an approximately equal number of poems in each, and often with an equal distribution of distinctive "types" of poems such as sestinas, dramatic monologues, or the Traveler's Vade Mecum series.

Here, I'm relaxing into a more organic order, but still with a consistent goal of at least twenty pages per section. Collections benefit from veering longer, unless they are organized around a singular narrative or speaker. Also, when a poet considers the possibility of a hardback run, she has to be mindful of creating a book thick enough to justify those physical materials."

Are you somebody who has a concept for the collection and builds-up to it or do you just write poems and see where they take you?

"Often, I have misguided ideas along the way about what a collection of poetry can be "about." I'm both tempted by working on series and sequence, yet ultimately reluctant to commit to any poetry collection whose themes can be summarized in one or two sentences. So I write a lot, and I discard a lot; I have a book's worth of unpublished poems dating back a decade. There is usually a discernible tipping point, though, when I transition from drafting singular poems to feeling like a book is on its way. From there, the poem production often comes faster because I'm writing into an idea. This is part of the reason that creative residencies (Virginia Center for the Creative Arts, the Millay Colony, Jental Artist Residency, etc.) can be so valuable: an organic process, consolidated into just one calendar month."

You set the bar rather high last time - do you feel any pressure (personal or outside) to better it?

"My goal is to do something different with each collection. If there's one thing I'd love to think, looking back on a lifetime of work, it's that 'She never gave us the easy poems. She never coasted.'

But in traveling from writing sestinas to prose-poems, for example, I'm redefining the landscape of my work. That is a liberating approach in terms of clearing a 'bar.' That's a challenging approach in that I feel I have to re-query and re-develop an audience for my poems each time; a journal that loved the work from a previous project might turn this work down flat. A trusted reader might no longer be a match. I don't think a poetry culture's aesthetics get better or worse over time, per se, but they certainly change. The poems you see welcomed now are not the poems that would have been celebrated twenty years ago. That's fine by me—you can't cling to a fixed definition of what is 'poetic.'"

You can find out more about Sandra at,

sbeasley.blogspot.co.uk

THE ROAD TO CLEVEDON PIER

A Competition & Anthology

In launching the Hedgehog Poetry Press, we thought the traditional Anthology Competition would be as good a way as any to find some poets to love and publish. Needless to say we were inundated and choosing a winner was seriously difficult. In the end, Victoria Richards was somebody who's poetry just wouldn't let go, and along with our two Highly Commended Runners-up, Sarah Thomson and Matt Duggan, we were many kinds of pleased.

The anthology of the competition of the long list, is of course available, in all good bookshops and a few bad ones too, but we thought it only proper to share the Top 3 along with a quick Q&A with each of the winners.

I WEAR MY KEYS LIKE A GLOVE

Victoria Richards

I wear my keys like a glove
as we walk, hand in
hand, feet crackling
over leaves. Their
metal kiss like armour,
heavy brass my bayonet.
Their supine edges are
knives I'll use to
protect you in this forest
of gold and green, and
a faraway tree that spills
spell-words like Silky and
Moon-Face and the riotous,
crashing Saucepan Man, and
Jo and Bessie and Fanny –
wisha-wisha-wisha.
Here, we are both six.

"Look, a cave." You point
to the darkest trees and I see
an ordinary man, in
ordinary clothes, standing
ordinarily. I see a monster,
a golem waiting in the woods.
and – my heart is a rabbit.
I draw you closer, move
my hand to the side of your
head to remind myself
of your softness.

I force your small legs
faster
faster
faster
until we fly. As we pass him
I cover your ears, lest
you drown in his siren song
of loneliness and need and
wanting, and my keys
are solid
in my hand.

Winning Poet: Victoria Richards

Can you tell us what the inspiration for the poem was?

"I was walking home from school through the forest with my daughter, who's five, and became creepingly aware of how small she was - and how little I had on me to protect her. I think women are very aware of their vulnerability - we automatically take precautions, such as holding our keys in clenched fingers if we walk alone at night. We don't even think about it."

When did you write it and where?

"I wrote it on the Tube to work, on the 'notes' section of my iPhone. Most of my poems start out as first drafts in that way. It's one of the only times I have to sit still and to think."

What are you currently writing and what are your forthcoming plans?

"I have been working on both a novel and a poetry collection. I'm in the process of editing both and hope that one day they'll fly out into the world and make successes of themselves."

MERCY

Sarah Thomson

In the Sunday sunlight late afternoon
Drug dazed from pain days seeking mercy
Heard that Cornell Campbell reggae tune
Dip my aching head into the icy sea

Out on the streets, into the unknown
Drug dazed from pain days seeking mercy
Up and down steps in the alley alley oh
Dip my aching head into the deep blue sea

Found a path with a bench where I could sit
Drug dazed from pain days seeking mercy
By abandoned buildings and a lamp unlit
Dip my aching head into the icy sea

Passing by the undergrowth where wildlife creeps
Drug dazed from pain days seeking mercy
I made a quick retreat, in fear of sudden leaps
Dip my aching head into the deep blue sea

Back where the blue coats walked by the wall
Drug dazed from pain days seeking mercy
Down the hill wind-blown the Hope & Anchor
Dip my aching head into the icy sea

Heading for the harbour dodging all the cars
Drug dazed from pain days seeking mercy
Past the apartments' balconies and bars
Dip my aching head into the deep blue sea

There on the boardwalk in between the barges
Drug dazed from pain days seeking mercy
There amongst the watercress and frost grey fishies
Dipped my aching head into the icy sea
Dipped my aching head into the deep blue sea

Highly Commended: Sarah Thomson

Can you tell us what the inspiration for the poem was?

"I'd had a really bad few days with pain in the neck/head but after lots of painkillers began to feel a bit better so went out to Rocotillos, The Triangle, Bristol for a cheeky cappuccino followed by a walk to the harbour. While I was in the café they played Cornell Campbell 'Have some Mercy' - you'll have to read the poem to get the rest of the story..."

When did you write it and where?

"I wrote it over the next few days at home in Bristol. Couldn't get the rhythm right at first but then I realised it needed a reggae beat, like the song that inspired it."

What are you currently writing and what are your forthcoming plans?

"I've got a few poems under development not least of which is a 'cult' poem about a Hedgehog! My ambition is to get a collection published and so I'll definitely be entering the Hedgehog Press collection competition. Not all of the poems will be about Hedgehogs though..."

WALKING WITH COLERIDGE IN CLEVEDON

Matt Duggan

On the day the first snow- flakes fell
along a muddied jigsaw shore,
slim boats lined with black blushed tails
smeared grit on brown labyrinth floor.
Path of tobacco and crosses in dead oak
matted with feathers and yellow moss
on waters where lost epiphanies float
above the slewed ringlets in polished frost.

I saw the painting of that man from Ottery
following him along the small palms of frozen sand,
beneath a jacinth coloured moon this wreckage of moonlight –
a circled sinew of bloated white rain.
Vinegar trails in a child's frosty hands
like lines of wax embalmed into cemented snow,
grass verge is a train track rustic and twinned
where a balaclava covered chip-fryer is shivering.

Close to a distant pier with green shining railings
a charred black orchid casted out at sea
vast cloudless sky sailing in dark colours
that can only hear an ocean stopping to breathe.
Car engine coughing among the mists of warming sleet
like fish-hooks that sway in dull twilight;
Winters canvas swallowing pin pricks of zenith light,
that shined on the children playing hopscotch on broken glass.

Highly Commended: Matt Duggan

Can you tell us what the inspiration for the poem was?

"The Inspiration for this poem came from a walk I went on last year when visiting Coleridge Cottage, in Nether Stowey in Somerset, we walked across the Quantocks on a cold and rainy day in September then went for a pub lunch in Clevedon at the Royal Oak. I remember I wrote the first lines of the first stanza in the pub on a beer mat, just imagining Coleridge sat in the corner sipping his ale and then walked around Clevedon along the coastal walkways, and that's where lines from the rest of the poem seemed to just fall into place."

When did you write it and where?

"I wrote some of the poem on a daytrip last year to Clevedon and Somerset, and the rest of the poem was finished when I returned home to Bristol. I always like to jot lines down on a mobile phone and then add them to a notepad when I get home. I eventually finished the final stanza late October last year and after a few edits I'd say it was completed at the end of November."

What are you currently writing and what are your forthcoming plans?

"I'm currently working on my second full collection 'Woodworm', which includes the poem 'Walking with Coleridge in Clevedon' , I also have two new chapbooks available 'One Million Tiny Cuts (Clare Song Birds Publishing House) and 'A Season in Another World' (Thirty West Publishing House) which is due this April 2018."

DEUS EX MACHINA

A. P. Middleton

For those of you that are familiar with Mr A. P. Middleton's crosswords, you will understand how pleased we were to gain his services for our humble magazine. It didn't happen without conditions though, and AP was keen that it would be a little different to the norm.

So I'm pleased to unveil our first 'Crossword' which is both fiendish and simple, depending on whether you know the answers or not. To complete it you will need to recognise clues, in the shape of lines from poems, and then to complete the grid with the name of each poet. It is as simple as that. Be warned that you will need to be well read and have read well to spot them all.

As for the prize, it is £50, no questions asked to the first person who emails us a correctly completed crossword to poetry@hedgehogpress.co.uk . If nobody does that before the 15th of May 2018, we shall declare it void and (if you'll forgive me the cheap and tawdry attempt at generating excitement) we will 'Have a Rollover' in the next issue.

I know, how more amazing can it be? Good luck...

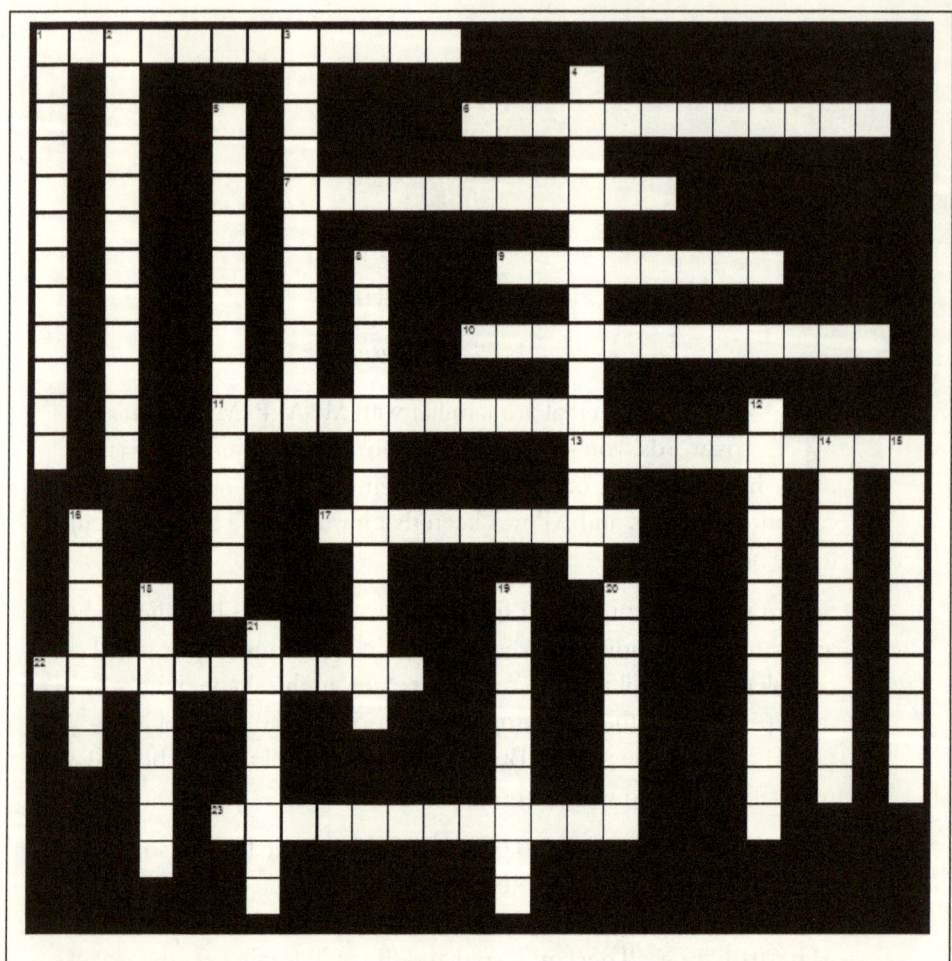

Across:

1. When the white flame in us is gone (6,6)
6. A paint brush gummed (6,6)
7. Today we made old people out of plastic bottles (5,6)
9. Big smelly bowel movements this blue January morning (4,4)
10. If you have to draw a line somewhere (4,8)
11. What passing-bells for these that die as cattle? (7,4)
13. When a Beau goes in (5,5)
17. Pike, three inches long, perfect (3,6)
22. My little sister, arriving quietly with your empty hands (5,6)
23. When the coffee-house war turns real (6,6)

Down:

1. It stretches out its feet (6,6)
2. On longer evenings (6,6)
3. Red as the guardroom lamp (3,8)
4. A flicker on the highest twig, a breast (7,7)
5. That autumn the newspapers were numbing (7,7)
8. Beneath whitewash, beneath brick, beneath mud (6,7)
12. Methinks the gentleman doth protest too much (5,7)
14. Slippery, mud-puddled (6,4)
15. The end came as I drove it down the road (4,6)
16. When you are old and grey and full of sleep (1,1,5)
18. It was a violent time. Wheels, racks and fires (4,4)
19. Your baby grows a tooth, then two (6,3)
20. counting the seconds to tomorrow (1,1,5)
21. The gorilla lay on his back (4,4)

postcards from the hedge
@mooseallain

www.ingramcontent.com/pod-product-compliance
Lightning Source LLC
Chambersburg PA
CBHW060530080526
44586CB00012B/685